Counseling
Is A Community Or Village Enterprise

THE SUB-CLINICAL THERAPIES
In Counseling Today
(An Igbo-African Perspective)

Igwebuike (Unity is Strength) Series

First Edition

Fr. Greg Udo Njoku, C. S. Sp

Counseling
Is A Community Or Village Enterprise

For ordering information, permission, or questions:
Fr. Greg Udo Ujoku
UBUNTU Enterprises
205 Northeast 2nd Street
Miami, Florida 33132
(305) 533-1800 office
(305) 533-1700 fax

Contents

Chapter One

Chapter Two

i

Chapter Three

Chapter Four

Dedication

This book is dedicated to
Barry University,
Miami, Florida
My Alma Mater

Acknowledgments

I most gratefully acknowledge the endearing love and concern shown me by our noble secretaries: Stella Carroll of the Department of Theology and Barbara Heffernan of the School of Counseling.

With love and gratitude, I acknowledge the role that one of my own confreres Fr. Eugene Uzukwu, C. S. Sp, my formator and mentor, has played in my life as a writer.

My greatest respect to my honorable professors in Barry University for their sincere love for students and for their subjects, and for believing in my little efforts in their classes, especially Fr. Mark Wedig, O. P., Dr. M. J. Lozzio, Bro. Ed Van Merrienboer, O. P., and Dr. Alicia Marill, all of the School of Philosophy-Theology.

I am most grateful to my professors in the School of Counseling who showed keen interest in the African cultural value system which I often expounded in the class and so, motivated my writing this book. Among them are Professor Maureen Duffy, Dr. Richard Tureen, Professor Miguel Y'bara, Dr. Scott Gillig, Dr. Rita Sordellini, Dr. Dawn M. Shelton, Dr. Marilyn Volker, Sloane Veshinski, Joy Dermarquis, and all others whose unconditional love and care made my Barry University experience a celebration.

I must not fail to acknowledge Senator Hillary Rodham Clinton for her most inspiring book It Takes A Village to Raise A Child, which I consulted.

Lastly, I owe my dearest gratitude to Dr. and Mrs. Emmanuel and Naomi Nwadike, my benefactors who made my study of counseling in Barry and the writing of this book possible.

May God grant you all His favors in abundance now and in eternity.

Long live Barry University, Miami, Florida

Long live our Human Race

Foreword

In the Metro-Miami newspaper of April 8th of the year
2000 we read: "Dinosaur Experts From Around The World
Gathered In Fort Lauderdale To Examine 'Bambi' The
Skeleton Of A 75 Million Year Old Baby Dinosaur . . ."
The same paper revealed that several years after the war in
Cambodia, scientists are discovering with excitement some
nearly extinct Siamese crocodiles. There are also threatened
species of tigers, elephants and wild cattle, brightly colored
birds, previously unknown species of insects, all in the
Cambodian mountains."

An expedition by "Fauna and Flora International of Great
Britain" made these discoveries possible. My question and
appeal now is: "Who will make an exploration of our rich
Igbo-African approaches to counseling in the family life and
society with its inestimable ingenuous qualities possible?"
This native approach to counseling is at the very verge of
extinction since many of the present generation of Igbo-
families in towns, cities, and far away nations are now
strangers to the system.

Our world today needs a rediscovery of our nearly
extinct spiritual, religious, moral and social values for
greater effectiveness in counseling.

Father Greg Udo Njoku, C. S. Sp

Certain Terms Used In This Book

1. Traditional Igbos

This term "traditional Igbos" is used in this book to refer to the "non-Christian" Igbos who were called "pagans" by the expatriate missionaries who evangelized that section of West Africa. I refuse to use the word "pagan" here since most people understand it to mean "non-believers in God or people who do not know God."

The traditional Igbos of old were neither Christians nor Muslims. They were following the natural religion handed on to them by their own parents before the advent of Christianity. However, they were very religious, spiritual, and God-fearing people with high moral standards, all of which makes the use of the term "non-believers in God" rather contradictory.

Many of these Igbos embraced Christianity when the missionaries arrived in Southern Nigeria in 1884 and 1885. Today it is hard to find practicing "pagans" among the Igbos even though many of the present day Igbos are children and grandchildren of those non-Christians.

2. Traditional

This term has been used very frequently in this book as an adjective to qualify a customary Igbo way of behavior or belief-system that has endured from generation to generation.

The Prologue
We Africans, Celebrate Our Lives

As children of Mother-Africa, please join us in this book to celebrate our Black history.

Let us celebrate our identity, our traditions, and our cultural heritage as Blacks; as African Americans, and all people of the African root and history.

It is good for us to re-enact our history as children of Mother-Africa, as people of the Black race. Let us celebrate our philosophies, ideologies, and the beliefs that govern our culture. Since our African traditional family lifestyle is essentially systemic, our Black history celebration is therefore a cosmic reunion of all children of Mother-Africa.

That systemic lifestyle makes every African child not just an individual but a community. This is because he or she can only be named and defined as the child of the family, clan and village of birth; that is, as "Nwaobodo" (child of the village).

Yes, the human person is by the African social definition of personhood a "being with," "living with," and "belonging to" [1] (Elochukwu E. Uzukwu 1996). To celebrate our being and history as the Black race, we need all people of the Black race to participate. We need the participation of all other cultures and races since the Blacks live wherever humans are found. We believe in plurality. We believe in cosmology. Our language at this celebration of our culture in the field of counseling, is that of multiculturalism for all humanity is our brethren.

In our Igbo-African culture, the quality of one's life is measured by one's ability to maintain good relationship with others. For us Africans, "one is human because of others, with others and for others" (motho ke motho ka batho ka bang, a Lesotho, South African proverb). Explained further, it means "I am because we are, and since we are, therefore I am. I belong, therefore I am" [2] (E.I. Metuh 1985). In essence therefore, not to belong means nonexistence, annihilation.

One of the great heroes that we honor in American Black history, Dr. Martin Luther King, Jr., drawing from this African concept of personhood in his famous speech in 1961 said: "Strangely enough, I can never be what I ought to be, until you are what you ought to be. You cannot be what you ought to be, until I am what I ought to be" [3] J. H. Cone (1993).

To God be the glory in these our celebrations, and to all who will read this book, peace and joy. Amen.

Father Greg Udo Njoku, C. S. Sp

Introduction

In a general sense, counseling implies helping people to be functional enough to live harmoniously with themselves and with others in all human relationships. The Igbo-African cultural systemic family lifestyle is that approach by which the family because of its unique structure, is able to raise a child from birth, through infancy to adulthood in an environment that holistically promotes the mental health of its members.

Factors That Enhance This Objective

1. A Religious Environment

Before the advent of Christianity or Islam, the Igbo-Africans had been traditional believers in God the supreme being and in other "deities" of their land. They recognized and worshipped God as the supreme being, Chukwu, but also had recourse to some natural phenomena of great potent in the same way that the ancient Roman and Greek empires did many centuries before Christ. Thus, the "invincible Sun" was worshipped, and so was the soil of the earth from which all plant life springs. No wonder these Igbos referred to the soil as mother-earth, for, from the soil of the earth, man was formed and goes back to the earth at the dawn of his life.

The Igbos firmly believed that religious commitment to God and the "spirits" guaranteed the favors and protection of these "higher powers." As a people of distinctive cultural heritage, spirituality, and moral values, their lives, were modeled on these native ideologies through the centuries.

2. The Igbo-Traditional Society Embodies A Counseling System

Embedded in the Igbo-African system of life is, a counseling approach which emphasizes the kinship, and therefore, the interrelatedness of all the group, as a people of one origin and one destiny.

Their traditional religion and spirituality constituted a powerful resource in the moral upbringing of children and the peace and happiness of families. In today's psychological age, "such a support system would certainly encourage a healthy immune system for studies in psycho-neuro-immunology" (Scot Gillig 1998).

Indeed, the community spirit which pervades the social as well as the religious and spiritual life of the Igbo-Africans, constitute a formidable support for all its members.

Psychologists of note have also observed this spirit of oneness and mutual support in Black Christian churches. Thus, a recent article reports: "Black churches of various denominations create safe and supportive environments that foster therapeutic experiences for group members, similar to those observed or reported by participants in psychotherapy groups" [4] (Gilkes 1980; Griffith; Young and Smith, 1984; McRae, Carey, and Anderson-Scott 1998).

As will be observed in the chapters, many psychological theories like Bowen's family systems approach, Roger's client centered approach, Jung's strengths perspective in social work practice and the cognitive behaviorism of B. F. Skinner, vividly resonate in the Igbo-African lifestyle.

In this book therefore, I present a counseling approach based on my native culture which is more inclusive of many of the known theories of family counseling.

Chapter One

Spiritual, Moral, And Religious Beliefs Among The Igbos Of South-Eastern Nigeria

"Unless there is within us, a moral law and order, mightier than the conflicts which are outside us, we will soon yield to the forces around and about us"

(Dominic Dioka 1983)

Preamble:

The traditional Igbos of Nigeria have aptly been described as a "deeply religious people who are known to eat religiously, dress religiously, work and walk religiously" [1] (Onwuemelie M.O. 1978). Religion indeed penetrates every fabric of an Igbo person's life. It is from the religious life of these Igbos, from their attitude to life and their preoccupation with the spiritual world that one can best verify the sociological statement that "man is a religious animal."

As early as the first century of Christianity, one of the Latin Fathers of the North African church, Quintus Septimus Tertullian (AD 197), in his book "De Apologeticum" asserted that "the soul is by nature Christian (anima naturaliter Christiana). It comes from God, is of God, and aspires to God." [2]

In other words, humans have innate awareness of God's existence even outside of any prescribed religion. Humans naturally aspire to God as their origin and source of life especially in moments of crisis. To really grasp the traditional Igbo man's concept of religion, we need to reflect on F. Arinze's definition of religion: "Subjectively, religion is the consciousness of one's dependence on a transcendent being and the tendency to worship him. Objectively, religion is the body of truths. Laws and rites by which man is subordinated to the transcendent being" [3] (F. Arinze 1970). Thus the Igbos are fully aware of their need of this supreme being who is omnipotent, omnipresent, and omniscient and on whose mercy and favors they depend. Their response and relationship to this being therefore, is that of worship and allegiance.

In his evangelizing ministry among the Igbos Fr. P. Jordan (1949) wrote: "Every Igbo man believes that an invisible universe was in action all around him and that his term of life was short if he happened to fall foul of its expectations . . ." [4] Truly the above quotation most vividly captures the religious spirit and consciousness of the traditional Igbos.

In my research studies in the early 1970's about the moral, spiritual, and religious life of these traditional Igbos, I realized that it was because of this religious consciousness that they were able to maintain very high moral standard of life. Living in remote undeveloped and unchristianized parts of Igbo-hinterland, with little or no influence of the world outside their territory, they flourished in loving, peaceful coexistence among themselves.

As farmers, their livestock flourished in open compounds and their harvests lay in far away fields and barns, away from their homes. Stealing and other malpractices seen in the developed towns were unheard of there.

An Interior Hinterland

The village community of one of the interior hinterlands where I did my earliest research in 1972 as a student. Here, VIRTUES have their home. "The moral law within," governs human life. Here, nature was still untarnished.

These natives could still boast of girls entering marriage as virgins, undefiled. Anything called a crime in the cities were taboos there. There was no parvity in their morality.

Their well-formed consciences ruled their lives. They had no need of law enforcement agencies to maintain order, justice, and peace. Children were brought up with the same religious, spiritual, and moral principles that their parents and elders practiced and the cycle continued.

To be constantly in touch with this spiritual realm on whom their survival, their success, and peace depends, these Igbos prayed at all times and in all life circumstances. It did seem to me that every utterance of the people had some reference to the spirits and the ancestors through whom they approached God the Supreme Being.

The traditional Igbos of old were less enlightened, less equipped than we are today. They were groping for answers to their diverse problems and needs. God became for them, a strong bulwark of support, an indispensable resource center.

It was in this type of quest that Carl Jung (1961) found out in his research that "there is a purposeful center of reality with which man needs to be in conscious contact for his full health. Jung observed that "man is seldom in sound physical and mental health, unless he can find some way to relate to this center of being whom he calls God." [5]

Prayer

Because of their intimate relationship to God, the traditional Igbos made prayer their life and their life was a liturgy of praises. They lived in very deep understanding of prayer as defined in the Catholic Encyclopedia: Prayer is "an act of cult or worship, by which man enters into communion with a higher superhuman, supersensuous being,

4

somehow conceived as personal, and experienced as real and present, upon whose power he feels himself dependent."

Igbo-Traditional Belief In Spirits

The deep and constant awareness that the Igbos have of God's abiding and pervading presence in people's lives stem from their strong belief in the spirits, since for them God is the supreme spirit. J. S. Mbiti (1975) acknowledged this fact when he wrote: "There is absolutely no question that Africans as a whole are very much aware of the reality of spirits. They address these spiritual realities or mention of them in several of their prayers." [6] Explaining the nature of man, a great Igbo elder said: "humans are incarnated spirits. We are essentially spirits, enfleshed." Moses Oleka (1974). Thus the Igbos often refer to little children as "mere spirits." When infants are having their baby talks in the first few months of birth, the Igbo elders would say that these infants are conversing with their angel spirits.

The Igbos believe that their dead relatives and great ancestors still abide in their midst, protecting them and conveying their prayers and supplications to God. One of the early anthropologists to Igboland, G. T. Basden (1966), was aware of this belief of the Igbos when he wrote: "But Chukwu (God) as he is called, is the supreme being and at his service are many ministering spirits whose sole business is to fulfill his command." [7] For these Igbos, every human enterprise is governed by the spiritual powers who reward or else punish defaulters in that sphere of life. In this Igbo

5

system of belief, there are spirits of destiny, of fertility, vengeance, of morality, and so on as evidenced in ancient Greek and Roman mythology.

Ani

Among the Igbos of South-Eastern Nigeria, Ani, the earth deity or goddess is highly respected as a kind mother who intercedes for all people with other spirits and with God the supreme being. Everything necessary for life sustenance comes from the earth: food crops, water, plants, medicine, and materials for skilled work. Even natural gas and various types of mineral resources, all come from the earth. The traditional Igbos therefore, have great respect for the earth deity and also fear her displeasure. Thus V. C. Uchendu (1965) wrote: "Ani (the earth goddess) punishes unrepentant and hardened offenders and gives many signals of her displeasure. These may come in form of famine, pestilence, premature death, infertility in women and men, and low crop yield." [8] Testifying to the same belief of the traditional Igbos, Green M. M. (1964) said: "grievous offenses against the earth deity called abominations (NSO Ani) included adultery or fornication, suicide, incest, murder, and stealing. Since the consequences of these abominations touch all members of a community, communal actions are taken to see that cleansing or propitiatory rites are made to avert the anger of Ani." [9]

From the foregoing, we can see that for a culture that lives in fear and respect of invincible, yet invisible spirits like Ani who rewards good and punishes evil; who is both

6

malevolent and benevolent, people would do everything not to incur the wrath of these spiritual powers. Pagan sacrifices for instance, often have a lot to do with propitiatory or expiatory offerings made to Ani. Any abomination committed, defiles the earth and some sacrifices must be performed by the community or the individual to expiate it.

The Igbo-Traditional Belief In Divine Retribution

As can be seen from the traditional belief system of the Igbos, their fear and respect for the spiritual powers constitute a powerful restraint on improper behavior by people especially in things that affect the society or an entire family. The culmination of this awe of the spiritual realm is seen in their belief in divine retribution or what can be called African theodicy. This belief in the divine vindication of justice together with their belief in the natural law, the role of the spirits and their revered ancestors who are seen as custodians of the moral law and order in the land, constitute their own law enforcement system.

The Igbo-African belief in divine retribution is in line with the older biblical tradition where God speedily punished evil doers. Thus in Genesis 4:8-12, God cursed Cain who killed his brother, Abel, out of envy. One of the many ways of teaching morality in Igbo-African society is through the folklore. Two Igbo-folklore will illustrate this traditional belief in divine retribution.

Introduction: Igbo Folklores

The philosophies and ideologies of our great African ancestors were not documented on paper as did the Greeks and Romans in what we know today as Greek philosophy, but remained as oral tradition from one generation to the next. The moral teachings and spirituality of the Africans of old were embedded in their numerous proverbs, anecdotes, quizzes, riddles, and folklore. These were taught to children as they sat round the family tables after supper and at Village Squares on moonlit nights. In later years, as formal education in schools emerged, these oral teachings entered the teaching curriculum.

1. The Two Blind Beggars

Once upon a time, there were two beggars and they were both blind. As they walked along a path one day, the one on the lead stepped on a little goat horn, bent down and picked it up. He blew it loud and his eyes were wide open and he could see. In excitement, he shouted to his comrade: "Here, I found a little goat horn, I blew it and now I can see!" He handed it to his mate who in turn blew it and could see too.

The first man however was not happy that his colleague had also recovered his sight. As he took back his horn, he thought to himself: "perhaps if I blow the horn again, my sight will get much better, then I will not give it to my mate as before." He therefore blew the horn hard and this time lost his sight as in the beginning.

8

Regretting what had happened to him, he wanted to lure his mate into the same mistake, for all he had desired was his colleague's ruin. He therefore gave the horn to his mate saying: "behold my eyes are now brighter for blowing the horn this second time." The comrade well aware of his malicious intent, ran away, leaving the greedy envious blind man to his fate, which he truly deserved. The moral lesson here is that envy is not good.

2. The Fox And The Rat

One day, the fox was foraging in the forest and was caught in a big wire trap. A little rat came by and seeing the fox at the very brink of death from starvation and pain, set to work to cut the wires of the trap with his sharp tiny teeth. As soon as the fox got freed from the trap, he leapt on the rat to eat him for lunch. The little rat slipped off quickly and ran for his dear life! From a distance, the rat saw a tiger and turned back quickly to warn the fox. He (the rat) soon thought better of it and said: "this wicked fox wanted to eat me when I released him from the trap. This time he will kill me before the tiger gets him."

He therefore turned aside and hid himself. Soon, the fierce tiger drew near, leaped over and grabbed the fox and ate him up instantly. The little rat ran home, rejoicing that day, for his life that was saved. The moral lesson here is that when you plan evil against another person, it often boomerangs on you. We should therefore not bite the finger that fed us nor should we spit on the pillow on which we rest our head. Thus, we see how the Igbo-African belief in divine retribution is exemplified in those folklore.

These two folklore agree very much with the scriptures when for instance, the author of the book of Job asserts that: "though the wicked appear to thrive, that punishment always await them" (Job 20:12-19). In the New Testament Bible, St. Paul warned the Galatians saying: "Do not be deceived, God is not mocked. Whatever one sows, that, the person will reap" (Galatians 6:7). Finally, the English poet and dramatist, William Shakespeare (1564 – 1616), in his play "Julius Caesar" said: "The evil that men do, live after them, the good is often interred with their bones."

Now, when we consider the degree of wickedness, wanton greed, and envy that plague our world today, we can then see why these folklore and all such cultural practices need to be revived in the formation and character moulding of children and adults in today's society.

The Igbo People's Belief In Chi

Most Igbos, according to Arinze (1970), believe that "each individual has a spirit, a genius or spiritual double. This is his or her 'Chi' which is assigned to him or her at conception by Chukwu (the supreme being) and which accompanies this individual from the cradle to the grave. The ordinary Igbo man regards his Chi as his guardian spirit on whose competence depends his personal prosperity."[10] The Igbos often talk of their guardian spirits which is God's protecting angel assigned to each person for life. Therefore, in moments of danger, excitement, or surprise they readily invoke this guardian spirit or angel.

The Igbo belief in personal "Chi" would be comparable to Freud's "personal unconscious" and Jung's "transpersonal or collective unconscious. This consists of universal images which transcend particular persons or individuals, times, and places. In essence Jung points out that the spiritual needs of humans are more potent than the basic biological needs" [11] (Jung 1974).

For the Igbos, one's personal spirit is also associated with his or her good fortune or otherwise, as well as one's charisms. The lines on one's palms (akara – aka) are thought to be unique to each individual. They point to one's God-given charisms. The Igbos therefore say: "Ofu Nne n' amu, ma ofu chi adigh eke." This implies that even children of the same mother have their individual "chi" or personal guardian spirits and so, differing charisms. The children would be differently gifted in their intelligence, their tastes, and interests. They could have different temperaments and diametrically opposed views on certain life issues and values.

The Ancestors

"The ancestor," said Bolaji Idowu (1975), "is the departed spirit of one's forebears who stands in close relation to the tribe or the family." [12] The Igbos ask their ancestors to intercede with God for them. They try to live upright lives in order not to anger the ancestors or bring shame on the family or clan. The greatest treasure or value of an Igbo family is its good name or reputation. Every Igbo family would do everything possible to preserve its good name. For them, human beings are rated according to their good or bad behavior, thus the saying: "Agwa bu mma" (manner maketh a man). The Yorubas of Western Nigeria would say "manner is the beauty of all things" (Ewa l'ewa, ọmọ eniyan).

On his death bed, my grandfather was quoted as saying: "My delight and pride as I leave this earth, to join my ancestors and the God who created us all is this: I have in all my long life on earth committed no abomination that would plague my children and their generations to come. If I owed a debt of money to anyone, my posterity can pay it back; but if I have committed abomination, it would haunt my soul, and plague my children" (Njokuocha Nwanyanwumba). A favorite poem of my early school days on the importance of personal reputation reads:

> The loss of gold is much
> The loss of time is more
> The loss of honor is such a loss
> That no man can restore.

The tragedy of our days is that these moral, religious, and spiritual values and the practical ways of imparting them have been left out of life's teachings, and character formation. No wonder then, our society today suffers from moral decadence and is spiritually anemic. Science and technology cannot take the place of these spiritual values nor do they negate them. The "fun" and pleasures of our time cannot substitute them.

The unseen ancestors in Igbo-African society are believed to be part of their families. They are in fact referred to as the "living dead" for their living children and grandchildren are still conscious of their abiding presence in their families and so, invoke them for protection and blessings. "This concept certainly helps to soothe the grief process caused by the perception of the finality of death" (Miguel Y' Ibara 1999). The Igbo family belief in the ancestors is very much in line with the concepts of Murray Bowen (1984). For Bowen, the family is an emotional system composed of the "nuclear family." This includes the extended family whether living or dead and regardless of where they reside. All of these, said Bowen, whether alive or dead, absent or present, all "live" in the nuclear family emotional system in the "here and now." [13]

From the foregoing, we can see that the religion and spirituality of the Igbos are realities in their lives which surround their very being and existence and influence every aspect of their lives very deeply. If an event or incidence is of joyful nature, God is praised and eulogized. Most utterances of the people make some reference to God and the spiritual realm. All promises or plans for the future are prefixed with Deo Volente—God willing! Their deep consciousness of these spiritual powers like the spirits, the ancestors and God almighty, are powerful restraints from possible misbehaviors. Their firm belief in the rewards that God, the spirits and ancestors offer to the well behaved also motivate the people to live virtuously. In a way, "such a belief system goes a long way to bolster the underdeveloped super ego of people who would otherwise turn criminals, take to drugs, get depressed, or commit suicide" (Richard Tureen 1999).

As Smith Edwin (1969) puts it, ". . . behind every African belief and action lies a fundamental experience of something or somebody beyond themselves. Like a mysterious power which cannot be seen and is not fully understood but which is at work in the world. Accompanying this experience is a sense of awe and inadequacy, of reverence, and dependence."[14]

The Place Of Religion, Morality, And Spirituality In Counseling Today

One may ask the question "what has religion, morality, and spirituality of the Igbo-Africans got to do with effective counseling in general?" As has been demonstrated so far in this chapter, religion and spirituality form the bedrock of the lives of the Igbos. Religion and spirituality are to the traditional Igbos what air, moisture, and sunlight are to growing plants. These spiritual catalysts, religion and spirituality, together with the high moral standard that the

14

culture breeds, help to form the consciences of people of this culture right from their childhood.

In schools, in the village markets, in the farms, anywhere and everywhere, the Igbos are steeped in religion and deep spirituality. They are so aware of God's abiding presence all around them that they often say "if I hide my misdeeds from humans, can I also hide them from God?" The tragedy of our modern age is that the more advanced our technology and learning the more materialistic and the less spiritual we become. Science seems to replace the person of God to many modern people today. Science is nothing more than the work of man through God-given intelligence and wisdom. In giving that first command to man in Genesis 1:28 ". . . to subdue or conquer the whole of created universe, God gave humans the propensity for all that human intelligence has been accomplishing in science since the beginning of the world. Bringing in spirituality and religion into counseling is like invoking God's blessing on human effort, which we call science. We certainly need that blessing today to complement our counseling theories and techniques. We really need God's blessings to aid us in the complex problems we meet in the counseling field of today's world.

As grace builds on nature and does not negate it, so should counseling build on and ally with culture for greater effectiveness and more lasting results.

The Igbo-African Belief System And Its Implications For Counseling Today

It is a common trend in people oftentimes, that what they do not understand in other people's culture, they see those things with bias and misconception and so, misinterpret them. Our individual personalities, our profession or state in life as well as our background, influence our general view of things. Because of your limited knowledge of a client's spiritual or religious beliefs for example, you should not as a counselor jump to quick conclusions on these issues. It would be safer to ask the client to state how he or she sees, feels, and evaluates things from his or her world view. The values that the client presents will help you to determine what interventions can best soothe the case. When we go fishing, we use as bait, the substance that the fish likes as food, not what we ourselves enjoy most. The client's welfare is our priority and goal after all.

Various opinions from renowned authors in multiculturalism will shade more light on these issues:

1. "Counselors are urged to avoid pathologizing behaviors that are considered 'inappropriate' and even 'bizzare' among many people in the dominant cultural group in the United States without first considering the appropriateness of such behaviors from the client's cultural context" [15] (Kathryn P. Shimabukuro, Judy Daniels, Michael D'Andrea).

2. As Walsh (1998) has it: "religious and spiritual beliefs, significantly influence the development of the world views through which individuals perceive reality, and order their experience."

As a follow up on this view, some other authors said, "...This is especially true for African Americans who have historically depended on religion and spirituality to cope with adversity and oppression and to maintain a sense of meaning in their lives" [16] (Hines and Boyd-Franklin 1996).

Testifying to their advantage for both the client and counselor another group of authors insist: "spirituality and religion have been identified as potential resources in therapy for both therapists and clients. For therapists, religion and spirituality often provide direction and meaning in their lives and are considered guiding influences in their therapeutic work with clients" [17] (Anderson and Worthen, 1997; Stander, Piercy, MacKinnon, and Helmeke 1994). Finally, it is obvious that clients', exploration of spiritual or religious dimensions of their experience may allow them to make meaning of their past and present circumstances, to endure suffering, to retain a sense of hope and to increase options for problem resolution, healing, and growth for those so inclined.

The above opinions show that many psychologists especially in the multicultural field of counseling, are now coming to grips with the diversity of cultures and so, peoples' differing views of life. Viewing all clients from the same lens irrespective of the person's culture and beliefs would be as dangerous as a physician who prescribes the same medications for all the patients he sees in the hospital. Counselors have to see things from the client's cultural viewpoint too. This is because as one Igbo axiom puts it: "(nku no na mba, na eghere ha nri) the firewood in an area is good enough to cook their food." And we also know that the same heat that melts the butter, hardens an egg. It would be therefore inaccurate to generalize that heat melts everything that it is applied to.

As Don C. Locke (1992) rightly said: "Individuals or groups, whatever maybe their race, color, or creed, have their unique personal, social, and psychological background. Therefore, assessing the personality of every client, based on the single standard, namely, that of a white, middle-class-English speaking male; is unfair, to say the least." [18]

The Igbo-African Belief In The Natural Law And The Human Conscience And How This Belief Impacts Their Life

"The Natural Law is the reality of moral values as these impinge on our consciousness, says Timothy O'Connell (1990). For him, natural law is not something super added to creation. Rather it is creation itself, obligating and obligatory. It is coexistent and coextensive with creation. Human reason can discover this law outside of faith or revelation." [19]

The scripture, human history, and the magisterium or teaching authority of the Catholic faith, acknowledge the existence of the natural law.

A. The Scriptures

In his letter to the church in Rome, St. Paul argues that "since the non-Jews or gentiles do what the law of God says or requires without having the law, they are a law to themselves or have the law innately imprinted in their hearts (Romans 2:14-16).

B. History And The Natural Law

The concept of the natural law is as old as humanity itself.

1. **Sophocles** (496 – 406 B.C.), in his Antigone, refers to it as "an old and indefeasible movement of the human mind which impels it toward the notion of an eternal and immutable justice, which human authority expresses or ought to express, but does not make." Sophocles calls it "the unwritten, unalterable laws of God and heaven. They are not of yesterday or today, but everlasting."

2. **Heraclitus** (c.540-475 B.C.), a Greek philosopher, speaks of a law, which however much disregarded, is nevertheless binding and universal. It is something common to all, as reason is common to all humans.

3. **The Sophist Antiphon** (before 470 B.C.), a pre-Socratic writing states: "the edicts of the law are imposed artificially but those of nature are

compulsory. If a man who transgresses the legal code evades those who have agreed to these edicts, he avoids both disgrace and penalty. But if a man violates any of the laws which are implanted in nature, even if he evades all men's detection, the ill is no less, and even if all see, it is no greater. For he is not hurt on account of an opinion but because of truth." [20] This is very much in line with the Igbo concept of the human conscience and oath taking which we shall treat in the next chapter.

4. **Cicero** (106 – 43 B.C.), a Roman statesman and orator, talked of "true law which is right reason in agreement with nature. It is of universal application, unchanging, and everlasting. This law cannot be departed from without guilt. (It is a sin to alter it) Nor can one repeal any bit of it and it is impossible to abolish it entirely. There will not be a different law in Rome and at Athens, a different law now and in future," said Cicero. "It is one eternal and unchangeable law for all nations and for all times." [21]

5. **The Ulpian** (c. 220 A.D.) quoted in the Justinian Digest. "Natural law is that, which nature has taught all animals. This law indeed is not peculiar to the human race, but belongs to all animals." For the Ulpian, this law seems to come very close to the idea of animal instinct. In this case whatever

behaves, behaves according to its kind or species. The Igbos again hold to this belief that behavior whether in humans or in other species, is genetically transmitted. Thus the saying: "Obara anagh atu asi (Blood does not tell lies)."

C. The Magisterium Or Teaching Authority Of The Catholic Church

St. Thomas Aquinas (1225 – 1274), held that natural law is a participation in the eternal law which is the ordering wisdom of God. It is a dictate of practical reason by which we distinguish good from evil. The first principle of practical reason is founded on the notion of the good. The good is that to which all are inclined. The first precept of the natural law is therefore that the good is to be done and pursued and evil avoided. Thus, the basic rule of morality consists in the discrimination of good from evil. Without this, there can be no decision as to conduct, nor any obligation attaching to them. Conclusively therefore, said Aquinas, "no one can be without knowledge of the natural law or at worst, the capacity for it like in the case of an infant or a lunatic." [22]

D. The Traditional Igbo-African Belief In The Natural Law

"The Secret of longevity is fidelity to nature and nurture" (Igwe, Nnam okwor)

Asking the spiritual head and group leader of a remote village of my research study in 1974 of his age when I was being introduced to him, this great elder who was about 102 years snapped: "Why? I am still strong?" he said, "still able to do the little I can in supervising my farms. I still take some of my great grandchildren into the forests to collect herbs and roots for my patients. I have been a herbalist and a farmer from my young adulthood."

"As you can see, my sight is still undeemed because I am able to distinguish the herbs in all their shapes and forms. I do pick the alligator pepper when they fall from my hands to the ground. You ask of my age! I was a veteran of the 'home-front militia' during the first German War, about 1918. I survived the epidemics that decimated this entire region after that war. The secret of my long years is that I have lived close to nature, following the laws of nature. You ask about me, why don't you ask about those ancient hills and trees up there? What about those primeval trees beside the stream and the wildlife in those jungles of our sacred groves, how old are they?"

"Some of those plants and animal species outlive us humans! Have you ever seen any of the animals on treatment in your white man's hospitals, any of the plants? This is because they have been faithful to the laws of their own nature and state. Symbiotically, they get all their needs from their habitat, rejuvenating from year to year through the centuries. Do we humans obey strictly the laws of our specific nature? Like those animals and plants, I feed plentifully on plants and animals, breathing the natural air of the forests around me. I too have flourished from year to year over the decades. I use the herbs and roots for any small ailments I may have, any little pain, and I do a lot of labor, which is exercise. I feed directly from the soil."

It is when we upset the order of our particular nature that we are dislodged. I keep the laws of the Most High, of the deities who govern our land and faithful to the precepts of our ancestors. We do not allow any crimes or abominations in our land. They are taboos" (Igwe Nnam Okwor 1974).

Thus, this village high priest and community leader that I interviewed, was in a synopsis saying that, the secret of longevity and of mental health is fidelity to nature and nurture. Therefore, if one both nurtures himself on natural good food without upsetting his chemical, emotional, spirituality, and physical balance, one would have better chances of good mental health and long life if God so desires.

Nature

My posture with Igwe Nnam Okwor in 1974. For him, the secret of longevity is "fidelity to nature and nurture." He was then 103 years young and gave me his theory on "the Natural Law and the Human Conscience in the Igbo-African setting".

The Igbo Moral Code (Iwuala, Omenala)

The Igbo-traditional society has a body of laws, rules and regulations to guard human conduct in every community. The decalogue or ten commandments of God, Deutronomy

5:6-21, are all represented in this venerable code and more besides. Long before the coming of Christianity, the Igbos have possessed these laws. They strongly believe that all people have a clear perception of these laws according to their locality, with slight variations. The basic principles are still the same.

Pope John Paul II testified to this belief of the Igbos when he said: "Before writing the law on stone tablets for Moses on Mt. Sinai, God first wrote it on people's hearts" (Pope John Paul II, at the foot of Mt. Sinai on 26th February 2000).

Is The Natural Law Truly A Law?

Yes, someone may ask the question, "Can the natural law rightfully be called a law? As an officially promulgated law documented on texts, the answer would be no. Yet human experience does testify to the fact that there is in man, a force or impulse that coerces and truly obliges all humans to a right conduct and tries to deter them from doing that, which their deliberate knowledge judges to be evil. That the individual ends up in choosing to do good which is presented to him or her, or succumbs to the evil action which his or her conscience condemns, depends on the intensity of these two opposing forces and strength of will.

As a matter of fact, both in history and in the scriptures, the natural law has often been mixed up with the conscience and the two used interchangeably. Even the Igbo theology and morality often talks of the natural law, the bar of conscience, and the heart as if they are one and the same thing. "The important thing to note here is that this impelling, coercive force does exist in man and as a law" (M. J. Iozzio 1996). Denying it however does not negate it nor halt its operation, just as your denying the force of gravity does not make you fly. Such a denial no matter how convinced you may be cannot rescue you from dying if you should lower yourself from the staircase of a ten story building because you are in a hurry and cannot take the elevator to go down.

Unfortunately the Mental Health Program Centers of our day abound with victims of drug, alcohol, and sex addiction who perhaps inadvertently, had acted as if the natural laws had not existed. It is only in the program that most of them may have the grace to testify to the existence of the moral conscience and the natural law, when they are in recovery.

The Bar Of Conscience

Conscience, in Greek philosophy, refers to "the experience of self awareness in the forming of one's moral judgment. It is that awareness of personal responsibility which is utterly characteristic of the human person." Thus O'Connell (1990) said: "every discussion of moral values, every consideration of moral questions, has as its presupposition, the existence of conscience. Conscience is often taken to be a synonym for morality itself: the rights of conscience, the duties of conscience, what conscience demands or permits, all these are taken to be summaries of the human moral enterprise.

From the Christian viewpoint, conscience is God's law written in our hearts. It is the voice of God addressing us internally. As humans, we all possess that 'innate capacity for moral reflection called Synderesis in Greek.' By our nature, we possess a habitual grasp of the basic principles of morality. These moral principles according to Thomas Aquinas (1225 – 1274) are always there at the back of our minds. When we approach moral decision making, these principles are brought forward to be applied in forming moral judgment about the rightness or wrongness of our behavior" [23] (Timothy E. O'Connell 1990).

The Human Conscience As The Igbos See It

"Conscience is taken from two Latin terms, con (with) and scientia (knowledge). As a word therefore, conscience means knowledge had in conjunction with another, that other being God. Etymologically conscience for the Igbos means Izuchi, that is, a whisper or quiet deliberation that one had with God. It is a whisper within an individual heart, which God alone hears and knows of. Izu mu na chim (my whisper or quiet discussion with my God)" (Julius Obilor Njoku 2000).

The Igbos see the conscience like a locked chest or treasure box, whose keys are held only by God and the individual who has this heart. Thus the Igbo name, Amaobi (who knows the heart of another?). Chimaobi – God alone knows the heart. Sometimes the Igbos use the word "heart" to refer to the conscience and vice versa. For instance, Izunobi – secrets are known only to an individual heart.

In Igbo-traditional oath taking, to discover the truth about a missing item or the boundary of a land for example, the Igbos see the human conscience and heart as the last court of judgment and the arbitrator of justice. They believe that if a person swears falsely in a village group, if humans do not detect the falsehood and convict the person, that God who is party to that individual's heart and conscience would through the operation of the conscience, convict the liar by giving him or her no peace until the truth is told. Here, the understanding is that the voice of conscience takes over after the person has finished with the group, gnawing the culprit to stand for the truth.

In such cases, the Igbo-Christians would say that the person died for lying to the Holy Spirit of God. This is what Christians believe to have happened among the first century Christians in Acts 5:1-11. The apostle Peter warned the couple Ananias and Saphira of lying to the Holy Spirit and they both were self convicted by their conscience and died.

In Igbo-traditional oath taking, conscience is concretely personified as the god "nemesis" who dispatches fitting punishment to the individual who lied. Thus they say, "If you lie to your fellow human beings, you can't lie to your own conscience for no one can outrun his or her shadows. Your conscience follows you wherever you go." Nemesis is sure to catch up with the offender (Chief Edward Ihejirika 2000). For the Igbos therefore, "nemesis" or the conscience personified, serves as a law enforcement system. Nobody can evade it nor can anyone bribe it. It is no respecter of persons. It does not ask of your birth. Nor is he interested in your race. The human conscience exists simply to execute justice if it is truly a healthy conscience (Francis U. Njoku 1976).

Conscience And Our Modern Society

The conscience and reason are among the moral and intellectual powers in man that reveal more of his likeness to God, and man's sharing in the divine nature. In our extremely materialistic society of today, the inordinate quest for comfort and pleasure has perverted the conscience of many. Some people are now proudest of things that they should be ashamed of if truly their conscience and reason operate on genuine morality. For some people today, whatever one feels pleasurable to do, is morally good as if humans are to be guided by feelings outside the operation of healthy conscience and reason. For many others, human behavior should be left to individual conscience. The question then is, supposing it is a warped and depraved conscience? Supposing the traffic laws were to be left to individual discretion? Then, we would have a well-organized confusion on the roads. And what would be the situation if we should abolish all state laws and leave the rules and constitutions of institutions at the mercy of individual whims and caprices!

We need to remind ourselves of the fact that bereft of God's grace, man is by nature selfish. That perpendicular pronoun "I" governs the natural man. Therefore, without the grace of God, the prompting of the Holy Spirit, or some modicum of altruism and patriotism, all that exists in most human beings is selfishness: I, I, my time, my comfort, my convenience, my opinion, and how much I have to gain or lose and what it has got to do with me and mine.

The Igbo-society and culture therefore, trains the child from babyhood to learn that he/she is only a part of a larger community. That there are other siblings sharing his or her parents with him or her. That there are other father figures and mother figures in the extended family to whom he/she owes loyalty, duty, respect, and love. The child is trained to feel this incompleteness without all the others that make up the family, the clan, the society. The child is made to know and believe that all others around him or her have as much need as he or she has. To know that what is good for the goose is also good for the gander.

The President of the Pontifical Council for Interreligious dialogue at the Vatican in Rome captured this spirit of the Igbo-society when he said: "We all need one another. Interdependence is a fact. And when interdependence is not just tolerated but accepted, appreciated, loved and lived, it becomes solidarity or what the Christians call charity" (Francis Cardinal Arinze) in the Florida newspaper Metro Miami of April 20, 2000. The Igbos believe firmly in the interrelatedness of people and their interdependence. They depict this belief in names like uwaezuoke (no one is absolutely self sufficient). Nani mu ebila (may I never live alone).

The modern western system on the other hand emphasizes individualism, the individual's rights, and freedom of the individual. This overemphasis on "the individual" somehow promotes selfishness, egotism, and self-centeredness. And since human cravings are insatiable, the welfare or good of the generality is in jeopardy. Nor is the individual ever fully happy with his lot in life for as the ancient dictum puts it: "Armo habendi, habendo grescit" (The love of having, increases the desire for having or the more you have, the more still you would desire).

The Igbo-traditional approach in childrens' upbringing and character formation shows that it is easier and more effective to form children not to learn these bad behaviors than to curb such behaviors once learned. It is better and easier to guide the tendrils of a germinating plant to maintain a straight course than to straighten the stem when it is full grown tree and crooked. Where this guidance is shouldered by the entire family, village, and society of the child's upbringing, there are greater chances of success and permanence of character.

Conscientization Is The Solution

As the reader will discover after reading this book, the Igbo-African approach to counseling is indeed the answer to the complex malfunctioning in human relationships in today's world. This counseling approach can be summed up in a single word "conscientization," which is itself a training process. The human person is body and spirit, a psychosomatic being. In the Igbo-traditional society and culture, through their belief system, their spirituality, religion, and moral training, a person born into this society is given a spiritual bedrock on which his or her life is founded.

The process of upbringing of an individual in this culture with the rich network of interrelationships and a code of conduct to live by, guarantees an ordered life in both the individual and the community which operates on this system. Any slight deviation from the right conduct in an individual is easily noticeable in the family or community in the same way that a slight engine problem shows on the dashboard or raises an alarm! Thus, the other members of the individual's world whether in the family, the school, in an organization, or in the society, would promptly caution the person and rally around him or her and the situation is taken care of.

The formation of the moral conscience or conscientization, is like the proper forging of the engine parts by the manufacturers in the car factory. All that we do as therapists and counselors is supposed to be mere tuning or regular servicing of the engine parts. Supposing the engine parts had ab initio, been wrongly forged? In that case, there is not much the mechanic can do except to order new parts. Therefore, it is very vital that the parts be correctly and properly manufactured from the beginning.

Also for the car to render effective and lasting service, it is necessary that the roads or environment on which the car operates be in favorable condition. Comparatively, that well formed conscience needs to remain unperverted and unconceited for it to be truly healthy. It attains this state by operating always by the code of moral laws of the society, replenishing, and nurturing itself with the spiritual, religious, and moral values of the community. In essence, babies are not born into the world with their character already formed. That task is for the society that harbors the child.

Conversely, for an individual who does not have this bedrock of family and social formation, nor the moral, religious, and spiritual foundation, any slight stress leaves that individual like a crashed engine and so, requiring recycling and reforging, which in therapy is likened to a crisis intervention. This is what happens to clients in our western system who get back into therapy over and over again or into programs. Thus, the Igbo-African counseling approach based on conscientization in communal environs is a prevention scheme not a treatment plan.

Chapter Two

Counseling In The Igbo-Systemic Family And Community

"Every individual Igbo, is a community"
(Father Greg Njoku)

The Igbo Family

An outstanding Igbo cultural value on which most other values are in fact based, is the concept of "the family." In this culture, a person is named and defined by his or her family. Thus, rather than asking a person for his or her name, Igbos often ask of one's parentage, family, or lineage. Like the Jewish people who would say: "Simon bar Jonah (Simon Son of Jonah)," the Igbos rarely call a child's name but would rather say "Anna Ada Lawrence" (Anna, the daughter of Lawrence).

In many parts of Igboland, it is more common to call people after their hometown especially men. For example: John Nwa Obosi. This means John an Obosi Son, Obosi being John's village of birth. This is because Igbos perceive people as belonging not just to their parents strictly, but to the entire village or town of birth. Yes, the concept of the family is for the Igbos very fundamental. The family is the cradle of life; it is a domestic church, the first school, a miniature state, a microcosm. It is one's identity in the Igbo culture. A child is trained to be greatly endeared to the family and to grow up to hold the popular saying that "North or South, East or West, home is the best." The Igbos really love their families.

In life, an Igbo lives not just for himself or herself but for the family. Parents live for their children and children live for their parents, mutually. In the Igbo culture, filial obedience is among the highest virtues. The fourth precept of the decalogue: (Deuteronomy 5:16) "Honor thy father and mother, that thou mayest live long and prosper" is so often quoted by parents in the training of their children. An Igbo, therefore, sees himself or herself always in the context of his or her family.

Igbo-Community Life And The Family

As it is with the family, so with the clan, lineage, the village or town of birth among the Igbos. The fundamental issue here is the belief that the members of the community in any of the above groups have something in common, namely, a claim to direct or indirect ancestry with common interests customs, values, and goals.

As I had stated in the prologue of this book, a child in the Igbo culture is born into the world as a child of the village (Nwaobodo). Thus, as they dance and celebrate the birth of a new baby in the Igbo village, the women would sing a popular rhythm which says: "Onye nuru akwa nwa (bia x 3) Onye nuru akwa nwa bia ngwa O, obugh otu onye nwe nwa (whoever hears the cry of a child, should run up to attend the child for a child is communally owned).

Yes, a child is born into a village for the village, and to be raised and formed to be a worthy child of the village. When Hillary Clinton (1996) made the statement in her book that "it takes a village to raise a child," [1] that was an Igbo-African concept. That statement is a moral imperative for our world today and not just one of those sweet talks that people utter! No alternative approach can form a child more effectively. In the Igbo-systemic family life, what affects one person whether in the family, the school or community, affects all the members. People cannot be assessed or understood in isolation, away from the community in this system.

A concept of an individual in isolation from the family and community would be a monstrosity in this system. It would be likened to a tongue, an eye or leg lying all by itself on the road, not being part of a living human body. The interrelatedness of people in this culture is portrayed in proverbs such as:

1. Ofu mkpisiri aka ruta mmanu, ozue ndi ozo (when one finger gets soiled by the oil, all the other fingers would in turn get soiled).

2. (Ofu anya beba akwa, nke ozo ebeba) when one eye is wounded, the other eye sheds tears in response.

Because of this interrelatedness of people, the Igbo-systemic family therapy would involve the entire family in any treatment, even when only one member of the family has been identified as client. Gerald Corey (1996) agreed with the above system when he said "the central principle agreed upon by family therapy practitioners is that the client is connected to living systems and a change in one part of the unit reverberates throughout the parts" [2] (Gerald Corey 1996).

The family life by its very nature necessitates interdependence and interaction in relationships. The family systems approach, which the Igbo family embraces, connotes shared responsibility and reciprocity. The Igbos aptly describe human relationship as "a loving reciprocity in which the right hand washes the left while the left washes the right in turn" (Aka nri kwọ aka ekpe, aka ekpe akwọ aka nri). When the two hands wash each other mutually, it is easier, faster, and more effectively done than when each hand tries to wash itself. There's equity in the relationship transaction! This axiom is in fact, the golden rule of the Igbo systemic life style. Communalism is thus, preferred to individualism in this culture.

In the Igbo family therapy, the horizon of the relationships can be described as terminating in infinity. This is because it embraces not only the nuclear family present in therapy in the here and now, but also their past generations of bygone ancestors referred to as "the living-dead." At times, the Igbos can enter into very intimate relationship with strangers who may be of any race at all in the world and come to regard such people as part of and members of their family. It is in connection with this form of adoptive kinship that the Igbos have the saying: Nwa nne di na mba (Brethren can be found in foreign lands). The transgenerational therapy that Igbo family system practices was espoused by a few great minds. Among them was Murray Bowen (1976) who held that "emotional illness is developed in relationship with others." For Bowen, therefore, while the nuclear family may be the unit with which the therapist works in the sessions, the emotional systems of previous generations of the family are alive and well, and very much a part of the family and the therapeutic process."[3] The Igbos do not merely live with this awareness in the family counseling but demonstratively invoke their "living dead and pour libations to recognize their presence in their traditional rituals and ceremonies. The Igbo family system of life is a comprehensive therapy.

The Family And The Community, Living Or Dead; Claims The Igbo Child Even Before Birth

"For the expectant mother, the entire family and the community at large are with her in her days of pregnancy, encouraging, cheering, supporting, and providing for her. She and her unborn baby thrill the family and community as she celebrates her life daily in the expected activities of life, interacting with them all for whom her child is to be born. According to the Igbo belief system, the incoming baby is in touch with the ancestors but coming in time into human society as a blessing of God and the ancestors who are often invoked in prayer to protect their offspring" (Onuoha Duru, 1974).

At the arrival of the new baby and the naming ceremony, the entire extended family as well as the community, gather to celebrate and to welcome the child into the community. The presence of the unseen ancestors is greatly felt at this occasion. As the naming ceremony continues, the child could be given such names like Nne-Nna (grandmother) on the father's side, if a girl or Nna-Nna (grandfather) if the child is a boy. The Yorubas of Western Nigeria would call the child Iyabọ (grandmother who has come back to us) or Babade, meaning, grandfather has come back. The naming of a child in this way has to do with both the loving fondness that Africans have for parents and grandparents and also their belief in reincarnation. Children are usually very proud to be so named in the family and such children are often pampered in a way.

The very gesture by which the elders at the ceremony come to greet the baby is that of loving respect and admiration. This is because the baby is seen as a reincarnation of their bygone ancestors as all the adults are believed to be. As will be treated in the chapter on the great Igbo-African rites of passage, every stage of the psychosocial development of the child is celebrated and ritualized, not only by the nuclear family, but by the entire community with that deep awareness of the role and ever abiding presence of the ancestors. This is what Bowen calls the "emotional oneness of the family, both the living and the dead".

The synergistic impact of these never ebbing stream of interaction of people in the Igbo family system is so powerful, that it heals all ailments of mind and body, resolves conflicts and diffuses stress, no matter their intensity. It is in this context of strong communal interaction that the Igbos declare that: ikere-ukwu hara otu na ndi muo nwezi oso (when the footsteps of matching people strike in unison, even the malevolent spirits do take to flight). In other words, unity and mutuality in action surmounts all obstacles and resolves all conflicts. This is because the combined effect of mutual interaction of people is always greater than the sum of individuals' solitary operations. The beauty and strength of this system of relationship is that everyone is helped to have a warm sense of belonging, of being needed and useful in the sharing of life's responsibilities. Nobody is marginalized, cheated, or debased. The "I" is subsumed in the "we".

In the many communal activities involving various rituals and ceremonies of birth, death, marriage engagement, settlement of disputes, and so forth, people go through emotional physical and spiritual experiences. They attain great spiritual renewal, which instills faith, hope, and greater love for God and neighbor. They are enriched behaviorally as these communal interactions constitute very powerful informal education scheme in diverse fields of endeavor. It is really in this context that the common axiom: ikwu amaghi ibe ezi ya (whoever does not know or understand the facts, schemes, and techniques of life, learns from, and is taught by others) is applicable.

These learning and healing processes are both formative and informative. Members who participate in these exercises go home revitalized, rejuvenated, recreated, healed, and enriched in diverse ways. In general, people are never the same after participating in these "love-sharing" exercises. All their shouting singing and dancing, their jokes, hugs and greetings do a lot to disperse hypertension and other stress related ailments. Many foreign visitors to Africa have in their writings described the Igbos as "industrious, painstaking, yet jolly-going tribe who celebrate their lives." The truth about their celebration of life is that these exercises are effective group therapy, which goes on imperceptibly fostering emotional healing and accounting for their great longevity especially in past generations.

Community-Spirit, And Singleness Of Purpose, Overcomes Every Difficulty

Once, I had this wonderful experience out here in the United States, of ministering to the residents of a large rehabilitation center for people with diverse forms of physical, spiritual, and emotional as well as psychiatric problems and diseases, for some years. My major strategy in that helping ministry or apostolate as I called it, was based on this synergistic interaction of people in various activities that can enhance their physical and spiritual healing and growth.

Their day included morning prayers, spiritual reflection, and shared individual words of encouragement, of motivation, empowerment, and admonitions. These were punctuated with songs and praises in which participants danced and clapped as they beat the heavy sensational

42

African rhythms. There were ample opportunities for individual counseling sessions and individual confessions. It was in that ministry that I realized for the first time in my many years of priestly ministry that many of the faithful that we deal with in the confessions and spiritual directions are more of patients than penitents. The church mainly addressed issues on morality and spirituality. Professional counseling and psychology has now opened my horizon to greater realities in human life.

In the shared intercessory prayers in this rehab center, people poured out their hearts in petitions, thanksgiving, and complaints in whatever way they felt, to God. They learned to bring everything of their lives to God in prayer. Participants took their turns in sharing discussions in which people opened their minds to the group members and got wonderful feedback from other members. It was open confession and indeed group therapy.

We had liturgical worship, and shared meals together. We had picnics, recreation or games. Singing practice and music appreciation were always done with great exhilaration. Together with God's shower of blessings in prayer and in all these activities, the interaction of people in that singleness of purpose, loving acceptance of one another, wrought much healing in participants, from inside out. Even the mentally disturbed people who joined our exercises were never violent as would be expected. As one of the members once said: "the moment you join the activities, you forget that you had any problems whatsoever and end up staying longer than you first bargained." Thus, their praise of God wrought inner-healing which they audibly expressed in songs and dances.

In general, these group interactions dispelled fear, worries, and anxiety in people, instilling courage and enthusiasm in participants, and enhanced the spirit of endurance and perseverance. Two Igbo axioms explain the secret of these community exercises and their effectiveness as opposed to individual undertakings. The Igbos say:

1. Onwu adi otutu n'anwu, adighi atu ujo (nobody is frightened by death when it is to be embraced communally or as a group).

2. Ibu adi otutu ebu, adighi anyi alu (a load borne by many people is never heavy).

It is the community spirit that dispels that fear, encourages the weak and sweetens the burden. Moreover, the variety of ideas, resources and individual charisms that people bring into group operations sweeten and lighten the ordeals and invigorates people and that unity of purpose propels them on. When the going gets really tough, they encourage one another mutually since no one feels lonely.

Conclusively therefore, we can see from the foregoing, how human interaction in family or group context, constitute a powerful resource and support for all its members, at every stage and age in life's rigorous journeys.

The Individual In The Igbo-Society

Indeed, the community spirit governs the life in the Igbo-society. This is very much unlike what we have in most modern societies of today. As a remedy, the individualism of our modern societies need to be balanced by what Adler (1979) calls "social interest." For Adler, one possesses this social interest when he or she can see himself or herself simply as a part of the human community. This is similar to the Igbo communal life where a child is inserted into the community from birth and is reared up in the society. This child is made to locate a place in that society, taking his or her own responsibilities and sharing the privileges along with other members.

Adler equated social interest with a sense of identification and empathy with others. "In this, one has to see with the eyes of another, to hear with the ears of another, to feel with the heart of another" (Adler 1979). Thus, the degree to which we successfully share with others and are concerned with the welfare of others is a measure of mental health (Sherman and Dinkmeyer 1987).

As will be seen from the Igbo family upbringing of children, people assess themselves in the Igbo culture by who they are in their community of birth, by what role they play in the society. This clearly is the measure of their self esteem. A person of high level social interest therefore has high self esteem and is highly recognized and respected in the society. The intensive training of youths especially from the pubertal stage in Igbo African rites of passage, is geared towards the realization of this high level social interest.

For Igbos therefore, a member of the community learns to live by, and to appreciate that fundamental dictum that says: igwebuike (Unity is strength). The family and society are for the Igbos the haven of rest where one finds support, where one is always accepted and valued for his or her own sake because one is part and parcel of the group, contributes to its welfare and so, has a right to its benefits. The worst punishment that can be meted out to a person in the Igbo-society is to ostracize the one from the community. This would mean that the person cannot share his or her daily life with other members of the community, such as going to the same market, fetching water from the same stream or well, attending social functions and ceremonies, or even sharing greetings with others. Such a person would be as good as dead.

A person can only be so ostracized if the one has committed a heinous crime like murder or proved to be an unrepentant thief. Such a person would be more like an outcast and would rather go on self-exile to some far away land than live in such ignominy in the society without being part of the society. An Igbo cannot live in a lonely crowd.

The Igbo idea of happy social life is well expressed in Mosak's (1977) view. He states that we should strive to master five tasks:

1. Learn to relate well with others, which is friendship.
2. Make our contributions to the society, that is work.
3. Achieve the intimacy, which is to love in family life.

4. Have self acceptance.

5. Be happy with yourself and with others.

"It is also vital that we should develop the spiritual dimension of our lives," [4] said Mosak.

Finally it was Sullivan who hit the point when he said: "personality has meaning only to the extent it relates to human interaction. How well you relate to others is a measure of your personality" (Harry Stack Sullivan 1962).

The above values are so beautifully demonstrated when in the Igbo culture, a man or woman meets members of his or her community or clan in a gathering. The visitor's greeting to the group is: ndi nwe'm na ndi mu nwe! (I am your's and you're mine!), then joins the group. Think about those words of greeting; "I belong to you as much as you belong to me". In other words, you are so dear to me and whatever be your want or problem, whatever be your joy or pride, they are mine and my preoccupation. And what I am and what I have, joys, or sorrows, merits and demerits, they are yours too. And they live these out in practice. Can anything be more beautiful in our world of human relationships, for any people who can live in such understanding! This is becoming a lost treasure in our world cultures today!.

Our Community Of Birth Influences And Often Determines Our Moral Standpoint

At the onset of life, the moral temperature of our family moulds us, and later the peers and associations that we keep in the society help to make or mar us. Still along the line, the impact of the important figures we meet on our life journey such as our teachers and other adults we admire, the schools, and churches we attend, leave their own imprints on our character and conscience formation. In life, whenever we are faced with moral decision-making, the voice of the community and of all those significant people and organizations we have met in life continue to re-echo in the depth of our hearts and inner consciences. It is, the personal response to this situation that leads us to good or bad behavior. In effect, it is what the community has upheld, what our peers, the institutions, the church or parents have taught us that we would base our lives on. What the community has amplified or stressed will echo more gravely in our conscience.

As Timothy O'Connell (1993) puts it: "Values are transmitted through groups. In groups, we find accountability to lead a moral life." [5] This is the core of the Igbo social life. A child is born into a community and for the community. As I said earlier, every Igbo is seen as Nwa obodo (child of the community) to which he or she belongs. It is the community that owns the child and moulds and models the child's character. The child imbibes the spiritual, moral, social, political, and economic values of the community. Whatever the child has and is, must be with reference to the community. The community's name is part of the child's name and identity and he or she remains an ambassador of the community throughout life. Thus we can see why my title to this book is that "Counseling Is A Community Or Village Enterprise." As a rule, where the community stands, there is the individual.

The Igbos can be called socialists in the specific sense that they live their lives, based on the welfare of all members of the community. This is very much in tune with Vygotsky (1994) in his socio-cultural theory. According to him, "social interaction especially cooperative dialogues with more knowledgeable members of the society, is necessary if children are to acquire the ways of thinking and behaving that make up a community's culture. Vygotsky believed that as adults and more expert peers help children to master culturally meaningful activities, that the communication between them becomes part of the children's thinking. Once the children internalize the essential features of these discussions, they are able to use their own language in the future, with the skills they acquire to lead them on" [6] (Robert V. Kall and John C. Cavanaugh 1996). Similarly, in traditional Igbo-society, adults and older peers provide children with the training and guidance that they need to pilot their lives as they grow into adulthood.

The Loss Of Our Ancient Communities And The Rape Of Our Moral Values

The Igbos believed in deliberation over matters, by all involved in all issues whether they pertain to individuals, to families, or to the community at large. Thus the saying that "one person's issue in the Igbo culture is everybody's problem." In all deliberations, they try to come to agreement and to speak with one voice. The tragedy of our modern age is the loss of our old communities. The rape of our moral values stems from the erosion of our human communities. When we lost our communities, we lost our power, our moral values. The community was the custodian and inculcator of the moral law and order. It was the community that helped to form true moral conscience in its members. Thus families and communities moulded human consciences and character.

The importance of the community speaking out with one voice, univocally, on issues is that this unity in decision making, gives power to the rulings of the community. The community is greater than the individual, the whole is greater than the part. No one person can hold the entire community to ransom. Thus, the Igbo saying: ofu onye anaghi esiri oha nri (one person cannot cook for the community). It would be suicidal for an individual member to challenge the entire community to a duel.

The Igbo community as a governing body was essentially democratic. There is a saying among the Igbos that a law is as powerful as the numerical strength and wisdom of those who enacted it. The community sets the measure and the pace for the individuals in it.

The Genesis Of Our Eroding Social Virtues

In the old Igbo communities, traditional practices and ethos passed on from one generation to the next. My father often said in his teachings to us and to other children of the village: "I tell you what I was told by my own father, mother, great uncle or aunt." This was the usual way he introduced his talks. With the growth of cities, of education, and modern technology, people's movement grew faster. Children often left their parents and homes even at their tender years to far away cities. Work situations set parents, often working away from their homes and so, had little time to be with their children. Communities were no more knit together as in the past.

This rape of the moral values and erosion of the human communities, was a global event, which swept through Europe, the Americas, and even the third world countries, each at a given epoch. Like the now extinct species of animals and plant life, the communities that preserved the moral values of old have become mere history, like the dinosaur. In most parts of the world, the more advanced in techology and scientific development an area, the faster have these values been eroded.

A few areas of the world who are uniquely attached to their cultural values have been able to preserve much of these values. Elderly people in all cultures continue to refer to these spiritual, religious, and moral values as "the lost treasures of their growing years." Is there any way that we can reclaim and regenerate these values, customs, and practices that guaranteed morality, law, and order in the human societies of old? The answer is of course, yes. If we can spend time, money, and human ingenuity in research, to preserve and increase fast dying species of animals and plants, we can also do the same with our spiritual and moral

51

values, without which our world is fast turning into a society where "man is wolf to man" and the end justifies the means.

The way out of this problem will be treated in greater detail in the next edition of this series. Suffice it to know at this point that it was the conscientious collaboration of the families, the institutions, organizations, and churches that propagated the now fast fading virtues and values. The inculcation of the moral values in children in the Igbo culture takes effect alongside their bio-psychosocial development stages. Right from a child's pre-natal existence, the process has already begun as I described in the pre-naming rites of a baby in Igbo community.

The child begins its moral lessons from babyhood under its mother, other adults who carry the child and fondle him or her as well as the baby's caretakers. Their lesson continues with the child's parents, elder siblings, and the child's playmates and age group later. The schools churches, institutions as well as the society to which the child belongs, each take their turn, and play their role in the child's moral religious, social, and political education.

Singleness Of Purpose

The common factor in this whole process is that each moral agent influences the child for good. This is what makes for that unity and singleness of purpose in the Igbo community. Thus the Igbos use such terms like: ofu obi (one heart), ofu olu (one voice or univocality), oluhara otu (when all voices sound in unison). In this way, the child does not receive "double" or contradictory messages. What one agent says, all others affirm. In this lies the power of the community and the secret of effective formation of the child's character. Not where parents say one thing, the society would hold an opposing view. It would be confusing to the child.

For instance, if parents were to teach their children not to steal or fight while the society would say: "You can fight provided you're not wounded. You can steal, but be sure you're not caught." In that case, the child is likely to follow the line of least resistance and would get into trouble. "In general, the problem of the world and social values today is that the family has her values, while the society has hers. The young people are confused as to which ones to accept" (Fr. Cyriacus Ajaelu 1998).

Once in a group session I had finished reviewing a videotape on drugs, alcohol, sex, and AIDS with a group in a certain program center. In my comments, I made no exception to the rule that they should keep away from drugs, alcohol, and illicit sex in all their forms. Suddenly, a teenage boy in the group said, "As for me, I use condoms when I do sex!" this fifteen year old boy, the only teenager in the whole group that day, was brought to the program by his mom, who was also there for our session. After the session, I saw the teenager and his mom leaving and I walked up to them and asked this young woman what she thought about her teen's remarks during the session. Like her son, she promptly said smiling: "of course, he is free to have sex, this is America." I was more scandalized by the woman's response than I was with her son's remark.

This is precisely what I mean by modeling or otherwise, muddling up the children. This is where moral formation and training in discipline is called for on the part of this young woman. Even in families, the father and mother could be playing two different but contradictory tunes to their children. Children like consistency in the rules of their training, otherwise, they get confused. As I said earlier, humans are naturally more inclined to go for the easy way out, for we are like rivers or streams of water.

An Analogy

A river in its upper course or profile is usually straight as it cuts through the rocks of its paths, having little or no choice than to flow down the slope. From the middle to the lower profile as it widens its beds with greater area of choice, it follows lines of least resistance in the rocks and starts to meander and to be crooked rather than straight. This also happens with humans in their life's journey. That indeed is the raison d'etre for the "African Rites of Passage" which we shall treat in chapter three. We humans, both as children and as adults, need laws, rules, and regulations to guide us if we are to remain faithful and honest to ourselves, to the society and to God. Rules and laws are for discipline, without which all we have is disorder or chaos.

In the Igbo community, the various moral agencies have the overall welfare of the community as their ultimate goal, and they work together and have their common table at the family gatherings, the village meetings, and in the social ceremonies and rituals. No moral unit or agency tries to run down the other. Each does its best to collaborate with the others. Since the child hears the same language at every point or stage, he or she does not get confused. There is no leakage or line of weakness and so, the messages stick and this is how good character and conscience are formed.

Obstacles To Good Character Formation In Children In The Homes Today

The unity of voices that prevails in the Igbo family and community that I have been tracing in this chapter which enhances the upbringing of children and their moral education, is in serious crisis in our modern societies of today. Many families in today's modern societies are dysfunctional from use of drugs and alcohol, from divorce and work interests of some parents.

Often times, particular or vested interest override the moral values in the society and both teens and adults are at a loss as to which voice to heed. The media says one thing, the churches, parents, and teaching institutions say different things. The problem generally is that individual or group interests and the utilitarian principle that governs many of our modern societies, do a lot to pervert and distort the moral virtues taught earlier in the homes, churches, and schools. Children as I said before, follow the line of least resistance and we also know that "forbidden fruits always taste sweeter," especially for these teenagers in their unbridled curiosity.

The culture of violence, of death, and immorality in today's modern societies are fed by the media and the television. They present these horrors as entertainment, thus, desensitizing their habitual viewers to their moral, spiritual, and other consequences. On a few occasions, I have joined children in homes, where they feed daily on these horrendous video games and other television programs. The scenes in these videos and programs that I felt scared or uncomfortable about because of their obscenity or heinousness never moved the kids. They were rather thrilled by them. This is most unfortunate and we are paying dearly for it in the ever increasing rate of adolescent and even infant crimes and other anomalies that we are seeing in the society today.

While many parents feel hopeless and helpless about the media impact, others casually state that "the media is not the problem". No matter the general view of people, the fact still remains that the lessons of the media create lasting impressions and expectations in the young, which are somehow impervious to moral scrutiny and even social criticisms. Nobody doubts the fact that we are products of our thoughts, words, imaginations, and of the things we view frequently. Constant preoccupation with nudity in thought and sight certainly make people lustful. Obsession with money and wealth could breed avarice in people. If not, why does the program for drug and alcohol victims discourage their frequenting the familiar areas where they had gotten their substances before coming to the program? "You eat with your eyes, before you eat with your mouth," the Igbos say. And if you stay too long in a barber's shop, you'll have a haircut. There is certainly no doubt that parents, the churches, schools, and the society at large, have a serious obligation to form children's consciences and help to mould their character in the midst of the poison of the media and other forces of evil in our world of today.

Reclaiming Our Fast Fading Legacies

Some Important Concepts In Igbo Family And Society

A human being is of such infinite value in the Igbo culture, that "the entire universe of creation that is not human, is not what comparing with a single human being." For this reason, the Igbos give their children such personal names like: Madu bu uba (humans are wealth), Madu ka aku (humans are greater than wealth), Nwa bu isi (children come first in order of priorities or hierarchy of values), Nwabugwu (children give or accord honor and respect). The community and society inside which a child's character must be formed to be a worthy son or daughter and emissary of that community to the world, is of primary importance. The community must be ideally good before the child that is to be trained in that community can be good. In the language of the Yorubas of South Western Nigeria, that community must be: Ile Ife (Home of Love).

But we all know that it is the human beings in the society that make the society good or bad. For this reason the Igbos say: Madu bu njo ala, conversely, Madu bu nmma ala (Humans make the society either good or bad).

Igbo Concept Of Time

The Igbo cultural view of time is of paramount importance for a good understanding of life in Igbo-society. The Igbos have two concepts of time, namely, the physical, measurable time as it pertains to humans, and time as it pertains to God called: Ogechi (God's time), which humans cannot understand nor influence but must wait on for its fulfillment. Physical time for the Igbos can somehow be defined as "a succession of events and incidents in nature's rhythmic cycle." Thus, nature opens its door with the light of the morning dawn and it is daybreak and the beginning of a new day, wholly unique in all history past, present, and future.

People in response to nature, open their doors as soon as they can see their palms. Waking up to the light of the new day, they follow their day's activities as they come in succession. They accommodate whatever events intersperse the day, till that day runs conclusively to meet the dusk, which nature brings to bear on all mortals, to give them the opportunity to rest their weary bones. Nature does this by closing her doors, (the firmament), thus, withdrawing the light of the sun, and humans in response, close their own doors to rest their weary bones till the next day (Michael Eze 1972).

Numerous events, whether historical, religious, spiritual, political, economic, cultural, and otherwise, punctuate the year and are often celebrated and ritualized in Igbo culture. These events thus, provide opportunities for family members as well as society, the church, and schools, to meet as groups to celebrate their lives, to effect reconciliation, to attain greater unity, harmony, understanding, and to grow spiritually, morally, and religiously. Where members of a family are having some misunderstanding, such occasions, blessed with the presence of the ancestors who are invoked in these gathering, have a very powerful way of effecting a great change in people, for good.

The Igbos Celebrate Their Lives

1. Greetings

In the Igbo-society, people meet in the homes, in the markets, in farms, schools, workshops, on the roads, at craft centers and so on. As I have pointed out earlier, the Igbos celebrate their greetings as they do with every aspect of human interaction and relationship. When people meet in the above contexts, they do not just say "hi," and pass by. They, in their greeting, dialogue, ask about families and life in general. They invoke God's blessings on one another and on family members, on life's projects and prospects. They give encouragement, advice one another, ask questions, tell stories, render epics, sing and dance, cry and laugh. All these are aspects of the greeting ceremony.

They are never in a hurry in performing these greeting rituals, which give greater meaning to their lives. This form of life interaction is what I would call primordial therapy. Such human interactions are very powerful forms of therapy in that they help people in this culture to go successfully through stressful situations of everyday life in informal, casual, and imperceptible ways.

2. Other Rituals

Apart from this general, everyday life pattern, the major stages of life passages are most meaningfully celebrated and ritualized, not just by the nuclear or extended family but by the entire village. These events include: pregnancy period, birth, naming ceremony, weaning of the child, teething, and the various stages of human growth and development that I treated in the Igbo African rites of passage.

On a special note, births, marriages, and funerals are the three great pillars of human life cycle that the Igbo culture celebrates and ritualizes in very significant ways. As some psychologists have pointed out, "people are most open to change, to reconciliation, and growth at such moments of rituals." They are solemn occasions, believed to be richly suffused with God's graces and the blessings of the ancestors who are usually invoked during these rites. In retrospect, I can now understand some of the reasons for the many rituals observed in the Igbo traditional culture. In effect, these rituals create opportunities for people to pause a while to reflect on the meaning of life and significance of daily events. These rituals serve as interlude to the hurried pace of time which is, itself, a flow of daily sequence of events.

If rituals are necessary for the Igbo culture that celebrates their lives, making time to attune to the diverse rhythms of life, then it is all the more necessary for our modern world and society that is ever on a "wild goose chase." I don't doubt that our modern societies are dancing to the music of their day! The only problem is that they can't make out time to listen properly to the music of the home and family, of the societies, the churches, institutions, and organizations and to know what tunes they are playing, so as to dance properly. The various entities playing their music do not even listen to one another. No wonder then, there is so much discord in our life stage today, for each plays to suffocate the others: families, communities, churches, schools, institutions, organizations, schools of psychology, or therapies each sees the others as rivals to be extinguished as if their existence takes from or threatens its own survival. Naturally each entity should enhance and enrich the other so as to have that variety which indeed is the spice of life.

There should be room for healthy rivalry among the entities, which makes for growth, creativity, and motivation. All we need is unity in diversity and not necessarily uniformity. Unfortunately there has often been so much strife, hatred, prejudice, spitefulness, and jealousy in human interaction and relationships in our days. Our modern stage of human activities, need to borrow a lift from the univocality that characterized the communities of old, as I described earlier in this book. The rituals, with the many prayers and invocations that go with them, especially in Christian families, create opportunities for people to reflect on their life's joys and sorrows, their hopes, aspirations, and disappointments.

The celebrations of births and birthdays, of wedding anniversaries, departures, and returns of family members, in ritualized ways, go a long way to heal the hurts of daily life, nurture the hopes and aspirations of people and unite family members more closely to one another. All these events provide happy occasions for thanksgiving, for petition and dedication of families to their God. When we recall that the Igbo Africans spiritually perceive God as permeating the whole of life realities, then we can understand how powerful is the healing effect of these rituals. In essence, God is re-enacted anew in the lives of all who participate in these rituals.

In their use of music and dances, of proverbs, jokes (njakiri), folk songs, epic stories, dirges and drama, the participants find solace in their misery, joy, fun, a sense of fulfillment, healing, and self esteem.

Igbo Cultural Music And Dances

The therapeutic effect of Igbo traditional music and dances should be no surprise to anyone who is acquainted with the poly-rhythmic structure of most Igbo tunes. The rhythms are often reproduced by the dancer's body. Thus, the head moves in one rhythm, the shoulders in another. The arms are moved in a third rhythm and the trunk in another and the feet still in another. Thus, the Igbo African dances both call for sharp precision and at the same time, makes ample room for freedom of expression for dancers, which in all, makes for a rich unity in diversity of performance.

Igbo Village Markets

The Igbo village markets serve multiple purposes. Going to the market in Igbo land is not only to buy and sell but also to have recreation both of mind and body and to have fun, and come home truly refreshed. For the traders who find their livelihood by buying and selling, it is a tedious exercise especially in a system where one has to bargain for the items sold. This not withstanding, it is still a lot of fun because of the humor that is so well embedded in the negotiation.

In general, all who come to the village markets are reunited with their extended family members who have come from other villages. People are reunited with their relations, acquaintances, boyfriends, and girlfriends, one's former teachers, patients, and people from all walks of life. At these local markets, people pay respect to elders and receive blessings from them. People celebrate greetings and reunions, enjoy great festival of traditional dances and functions. Going to the Igbo village markets is very therapeutic in diverse ways. Yet, this is a regular life affair since people must frequent the market averaging two or three times in the week or even more.

The Igbo-Community, Legal And Counseling System
(The Aladinmma, "that the community may be in harmony")

People all over Igbo land have their different ways of dealing with human relationship issues, so as to maintain the necessary law and order in their communities. In my section of Igbo land called Nguru – Mbaise, every village group has a large and inclusive bench. As a moral body, this committee or bench is made up of the legal and advisory representatives of the major social groups in the community. Invariably, they are zonal segments and communities and kinship units such as clans or age groups. The community leaders serving as judges and advisers, formed a regular recognized hierarchy.

There are also the council of titled elders who hold the village "Ofor," emblem of justice. They were both consultants and counselors, being proven men of high moral rectitude and had served as sages for their clans. The village or town court (Aladinmma) is held monthly and the village meetings, bi-monthly. The family meetings are held on weekly basis at the early hours of the morning of the day of meeting. Life exigencies and needs however, could alter this order. Villagers are usually excited to attend these gatherings, for on these depend the order, justice, peace, and tranquillity of the village and family life.

Issues Dealt With

All through the week, from day to day, people go about their daily life routine, but observing the issues raised in human relationships and interactions, in families, places of work, schools, churches, markets, and the society at large. Every form of human behavior that connotes cheating, injustice, stealing, wickedness, hatred, envy, violence, and so forth are noted, and could be brought up by an observer or a victim, for treatment in the village court sessions or the family or village meetings.

There is always an order of proceedings in these meetings. The claimant made his or her accusation and the defendant ascended a podium in full view of the village. Witnesses to the events or issues were required to express their opinions in support or disapproval. The cases are discussed and the judges held a brief discussion before giving their verdict on the matter. Accused persons were also free to protest or reject the verdict and appeal against it. Each village or community had a "body of laws," Corpus juris or laws of the land (Iwuala). In fact, the whole content of the decalogue or "the Ten Commandments of God" in

Deuteronomy 5:6-21 are well represented in the Igbo village laws and more besides.

The Elders As Community Counselors

The village court proceedings are not held to crush an offender but for the general good and wholesome health of the members. The Elders and Sages of the village take up the cases from where the local or village courts stopped. The court merely exposes and diagnoses the ills of the society. It is the duty of the wise elders, serving as counselors and mediators, to treat the issues so that they may be healed and eradicated.

In this connection, the elders meet with the people who are directly involved in the issues, and they mutually agree on how they would counsel these individual, usually on family level.

The Village And Family Meetings

As earlier mentioned, there are always village meetings held in village squares either in their Civic Hall or under the shades of trees especially during the dry seasons of the year when there are no rainfalls. These meetings are held to determine the right solution to disputes over land, property, or other matters ensuing from human relationships in families and the society. Rarely do villagers take cases to the city courts except when they have failed to settle them in their village local courts or in their village family meetings.

Among the Igbos of old, it is immoral to take one's kinsman or woman to government courts for as their saying goes: "One's relationship with a neighbor is never the same, after both have taken their case to the court and back." The elders would always advise the disputing parties saying: "it is a home issue, you are brethren" (Celestine Thejiere 1988). Moreover, not every type of case can be taken to the formal courts. Things that can be best treated in ritual ceremonies for instance, do not need court hearing. Oracles and ordeals still exist in some parts of Igbo land. Ordeals range from oath taking on Shrines or the Bible among Christians, to being acclaimed or disclaimed by the great elders with the "Ofor," the emblem and symbol of justice and truth. If the party that took the oath was not harmed, that became a sure proof of innocence. A vestige of ordeals in modern Euro-American courts today is the fact that witnesses and the principals still take oaths on entering the witness stand.

Community Work

People in villages often did their farm work and construction work in groups according to communities and age grades. Villagers helped one another in their work for an approximate return in kind or else for sheer charity and altruism or in that community spirit that made one person's problem, every other person's concern. Moreover, it is often a matter of reciprocity, mutuality, or symbiosis as the Igbo saying puts it: aka nri kwo aka ekpe, aka ekpe akwo aka nri (the right hand washes the left hand and the left hand washes the right) and both are much more easily and effectively cleaned.

As a rule, the people of a given community got together to carry out community labor such as road construction, or the building of a local bridge. Clearing the market place or putting up a new Village Hall. Part of one's civic duties therefore consisted in carrying out one's portion of the work of the community. A person's community in the Igbo culture was his place of defence, of refuge, and consolation in life and in death.

The Igbo Family And Society – Revisited: Family Reputation

The family image is at the very core of all social relationships in Igbo culture. The Igbo cultural family spreads out to the clan or kinship system which is itself an arm of the society or village. The society is of course, an arm of the national culture of humanity, in today's global village or world.

The Igbo African family operates on the crucial awareness that what happens in the family ripples out into the larger units, often with irreversible consequences that can either make or mar the society. The social life of family members in this culture lays emphasis more on the "we," "our," and "us," rather than on the "I," "me," and "mine." In this wise, members show great concern for the needs of others; their expectations, feelings, and wishes. An individual member of a family would, therefore, make every sacrifice possible, to preserve the good name or image of the family in the society.

Igbo-African Family Network

My extended family, celebrating my parents' wedding-golden jubilee. About 90-100 persons, to share one's life with is more than enough support system. Then, think of the synergistic impact of belonging to such a family network; emotionally, economically, and socially!

New Trends In Marriage And Marrying

In the whole field of marriage processes in Igbo culture, a new era has dawned. Marriage arrangements and betrothals as in the days of some of our parents and grandparents can no longer work in today's Igbo-society. Instead, children select their lovers and seek their parents' explicit consent and blessings on their choice in marriage. Even bride prices have remarkably been lowered in most areas of Igbo land, for high bride prices were never to the welfare of the young family.

Children's marriage in Igbo culture do not alienate them from their families of birth. Yes, children's marriage enriches and enlarges families but does not separate them. The keynote to the relationship of in-laws in the Igbo family can be seen in the Igbo axiom that "One's in-laws are his or her brethren" (Ogo madu bu nwa nne ya). Explaining this axiom, my father said: "When a person steps out from his or her nuclear family to marry from another family, that person is extending the family to coalesce with the in law family. In so doing, he or she is expanding and enlarging his or her family. The members of the two families ipso facto become brothers and sisters, fathers and mothers, uncles, aunts, nephews, and nieces to one another. This is the first stage in this fusion and amalgamation of the two families. Therefore, they have become relatives and as one family, they are extensions and prolongations of each other in a natural bond that should last, in life and in death.

Thus, the two families become relatives before they can become in-laws. If they cannot be truly relatives through love and understanding, then let them not unite because it is the marriage of two families not two persons, man and woman. The second stage in this union of the two families in marriage is that, having become relatives, they can now become in-laws. But for the Igbo culture, because of the depth of relationship of the two families, the English word in-laws, is to my understanding, inadequate here. If truly the two families united in marriage have become relatives, they can best be referred to as brothers-in-love and sisters-in-love and so on (Lawrence Anylechi Njoku 1982).

A Great Elder And Sage

"Ogo Madu bu nwa nne ya" (one's in-laws are his or her brethren) said this great Elder. In marriage, the two families and indeed the two communities of the partners in marriage must become relatives before they can become in-laws. Where this happens, they can best be referred to as brothers- and sisters-in-love and not in-laws. Love should govern and dictate family relationship and not laws (Lawrence Anyalechi Njoku).

A Reflection

I quite agree with the above elucidation of my father and his preference for the expression "in-love" to connote people, in marriage-relationship instead of the term "in-laws". The term "in-laws" has been in use from the dawn of human-marital enterprise till today, but human society and values have changed drastically through the ages. The ever-escalating rate of divorce and family-dysfunctions in our time may be partly due to the tendency of couples and in-laws to run so readily and easily to courts and to invoke civil court laws on rights and privileges of couples rather than endeavor to nurture the love-union which alone defines marriage.

As brothers and sisters-in-love (as my father rightly called the relationship), families and people who have become relatives in marriage, should relate in-love rather than in-law which encourages litigations and fighting in court and out of court. The guiding principle here is the fact that the demands of Law, are finite and transient, while those of Love are infinite and eternal. For instance, while the precepts of the Law may state that each partner give a minimum of one hour to playing and listening to their child each day, a parent's Love for the child compels him or her to stay three hours or more with the child if deemed necessary.

The patience, the service, understanding, devotion and communal spirit that should characterize marriage-relationship, stand so shabby at the bar of today's marriage-courts. After all, the marriage-courts will have fewer clients in a culture where marriage-relatives are brothers and sisters-in-love, rather than in-laws. Thus, the Igbos say: ala adigh nmma, bu Dibia ihe oma n'aka (A state of crisis and confusion in a land, is to the sorcerer's advantage). The horrible situation favors the sorcerer because people of the land would flock to his clinic on consultation, trying to solve their problems. This is what is happening in our modern marital system.

The Issue Of Divorce In Igbo Culture

Divorce is a very rare phenomenon in the Igbo family life and culture. That does not imply that couples are made to remain in marriage even when the union has become unhealthy, abusive, and dysfunctional. The above explanation by a great Igbo elder shows that the culture sees marriage intrinsically as a permanent institution. They work on a wellness model and invest all their resources from the inception to see that it perdures. One can often hear some elders at the "rites of introduction" of would-be-spouses in words like: "better look before you leap." Divorce is not in our marriage dictionary. It is almost a taboo. For the Igbos, therefore, before marriage, you choose whoever you love. After marriage you have to love the person you chose for there is no going back.

A Divorce That Never Worked

Once in a parish I worked in Nigeria, a couple, both of whom were in their mid-fifties, had some misunderstanding and their families convened a meeting to look into the matter. As the meeting began, the bride got up and announced that "the marriage was over, that all she wanted was to collect her belongings with her two youngest kids and to follow her paternal family home that day."

The entire group in unison said to her, "OK, take out all that belongs to you in the house." She did so, carrying out even items which everyone present knew could not be her personal property. The husband remained calm till the elders told him, also to bring out everything that were his, in case the wife would lay claim to some other items in the process. The man in jubilation went towards his wife and enfolded her in his arms and hugging her said, "Am OK, nothing more!" The case ended there because the wife also hugged him in response, rejoicing. The people present were somehow embarrassed, wondering why the meeting was convened at all!

The simple fact is that in the Igbo culture, marriage is a kinship relationship. It will need the agreement of the two villages and the couple concerned to break the marriage, just as it needed their mutual agreement to establish it ab initio. The families always work towards the loving preservation of the union.

The Igbo Family Systemic Cycle

"The Igbo family system is governed by a cycle of relationships and interdependence instead of independence. In it, every human operation is interactional, relational, and behavioral. Life in the Igbo culture is action, which is always in relation to others" (Chief Mike Nwadike 2000). Nothing that is worthwhile is strictly personal, rather, it involves other members of the family.

The Igbo family system operates more in the line of Salvador Minuchin's structural family approach. The Igbo family pattern is hierarchically structured with three subsystems:

1. **The Spousal Subsystem.**

The family relates first as husband and wife and have ample time to be close to each other and to their extended families. From the moment children start to arrive into the marriage, the attention of both spouses are almost always on the children. Their lives henceforth would be mostly, as far as this pertains to the children.

2. **As Parents.**

The second classification in the family is the family life of the spouses with their children as parents. This is the very essence of married life in this culture. A childless marriage will be severely shaken in the Igbo family life. Igbo parents are happiest when addressed or prefixed with the names of their children such as: Papa Sunny, Mamma Emeka. Parents see their children as the full realization of their personality, as extensions and prolongations of their being.

I remember asking a village elder, a new catechumen in our catechism class in a certain village, what he understood by the term "immortality," since we say that our souls are immortal. Smiling the man said, "What else is immortality if not that whoever is begotten, beggets his or her own children. That guarantees the perpetuity of one's lineage. I have no fear of the termination of my life, since my generation will continue in my many children," he concluded. The man did not answer the catechism question correctly but his answer gives us an understanding of how a traditional Igbo, views the extreme importance of children in married life even beyond the finality of death.

In that subsystem of the family where the parents with their children live as a team, almost all aspects of life that they can carry out together, are done as a team: cooking and eating of daily meals, house chores, farm work, most other activities of daily life. It is precisely under these circumstances that children ask their questions to parents, older siblings and other adults, and are given the life instructions and teachings that form their character. It is in the family setting and in the family upbringing of children in Igbo-society that their culture is taught to them.

Some notable anthropologists to Africa, Paul Bohannan and Philip Curtin (1971), were aware of this when they wrote: "Man and culture by which he lived, evolved together. The development of one, cannot be considered in the absence of the other." [7] In the Igbo-society, the customs of the family and clan must constitute the body of a child's primary knowledge. This knowledge is to the Igbos, what the Talmud is to the Jews. When most other things are taken into consideration, we have to admit that values, whether spiritual, moral, religious, economic, political, and otherwise, can best be indicated by parents. This is because these values can be interwoven rather imperceptibly into every day life event and activity as the children are being raised and they sink in and adhere to the children's lives and become their second nature.

Counselors, schools, churches, and other organizations can teach these values too, but no other group or persons can do it so effectively and with such "effortless supremacy" as parents. It is for this reason that the Igbos say: "egwu, amuru na nwata, ukwu ya na eru ala (a dance that one learned in childhood is characterized by the fact that the dancer is able to bend gracefully in rendering it, which is not possible for a person who learned it in later life). Most athletes, musicians, and sports men and women who have distinguished themselves in history, started their career in early childhood and this is manifest in their performance.

Again, in the parental subsystem of the Igbo family, the authority of parents is well defined and highly respected by the children. Even after the children have got married and established their own families, they still confer with their parents, helping them all the more in appreciation. "In some cultures, children are often reminded by parents from their tender years that they would all branch off from the family at different times to form their own respective families. They were however to do so always as branches of the one mother family" (Maureen Duffy 1998). In the Igbo culture, respect and obedience to parents, so long as they live, is never disputed. There is an Igbo proverb that says: Ọkọrọ anaghi aka onye kuru ya (the okoro plant is never taller than the owner or planter. That a child is never taller than the parents refer to parental authority and loyalty).

3. **The Sibling Subsystem In The Igbo Family.**

Many tribes among the Africans have been known in history for large families. Most families in Igbo land have average of six or more children. I have four brothers and four sisters, for we are nine children of the same parents. Parents and their children remain closely knit together throughout life such that the children's marriages do not effect a physical separation of children from their parents. Instead, children do everything to have their parents around them as far as possible, so long as these parents and grandparents are alive.

As siblings, children of the same parents are fondly knit together in loving and caring relationship. There is an Igbo axiom, which explains this fondly and loving relationship, which words cannot fully describe. It says: "anaghi akara nwata akara si ka okuru awa ọtọtara (no one reminds or tells a child to carry and to nurse his or her baby brother or sister). In other words, the child does this naturally, just as a mother is never reminded to breast-feed her crying baby, but does it naturally and lovingly. Even my translation of this axiom does not quite capture the intimate relationship here, as the Igbo words have it.

Siblings in Igbo families protect, defend, fend for, and love one another according to their order of birth. They virtually control the activities in the family as they progress in years, with the parents coordinating. They share out chores and duties in the home according to their ages in a way that even a three year old has some share. This sharing of work is a practical training in responsibility, accountability, in resilience, in teamwork and team spirit. In the final analysis, they are training to be fathers and mothers of tomorrow.

The training of children in the family operates on the principle quoted earlier in chapter one, namely that "there is no parvity in Igbo morality." It is this training that prepares the ground for any accomplishment hoped for in the future. In the training of children in this culture, there are no half measures, no room for mediocrity. The Igbo community does not tolerate indolence and complacency. The children are the mirror of the family in the community.

To justify this strictness and firmness in the training of children, Igbo elders would say: ana esita n'aku epe ama nwa ga eji ugwo (you will know a child who will be a shameless borrower, from the game of children in which they borrow materials from their opponents when they miss the mark). In essence, a child who is not responsible in little things will be irresponsible even in greater things. Therefore, there is no "softness" in the training of Igbo children.

Traditions And Rituals In The Igbo Family System

Perhaps, it would be more correct to say that life in the Igbo African family of old was one long therapeutic session, when we consider the traditions and rituals that punctuated their daily family life. No wonder then, they enjoyed such great mental health and family bliss that is so rare to come by again in our time.

Traditions (OMENALA)

These are time tested and honored practices of a people and place. These are modes of behavior, or way of doing things in the family, that have come to stay as a way of life for the particular family or group. Such ways of behavior, when maintained, create a memory and impression in the members of the family such that they begin to appreciate and to look forward to their repetition. The unique traditions of a given family identify them as being different from other families and for this reason, they strive to maintain them as rituals. Nothing thrills the hearts of growing children in the Igbo culture, as do these traditions which they curiously ask questions about and receive explanations from elders, on their significance.

A Family Example

In my part of Igboland in the extended family or clan, at the Harvest of the first fruits in the year, the oldest man in a large family collects a large quantity of the first fruits from the family farm. He convokes a gathering of all the families of a kinship group.

At the onset, he could for instance narrate the history of the ancestors of that clan to the third and fourth generations as he had learned from his own parents and great uncles. He then invokes the blessings of their bygone ancestors, pledging with all present, to be faithful to the moral laws, spiritual, and religious beliefs of the land. They would then share the fruits with some light meal and chicken soup.

All the food and drink taken at this ceremony are believed to be of medicinal and therapeutic value, able to heal sicknesses and diseases, infertility, and avert misfortunes. It is a meal of re-enactment with their God, the ancestors and with one another. On the other hand, any of the family members plotting evil against another or harboring grudges, is meant to desist from the intended evil to be able to take the meal and to confess and to reconcile with all family members. The event provides a rich forum for reconciliation and conflict resolution. If one should harbor grudges and plots of evil, with no intent to reconcile, but partakes of the meal, that person is, by the belief of the culture, bound to fall sick or even die.

Traditions Of Prayer In Family

While growing up in my family, I can still recall how my mother enjoined us to participate in the "family evening prayer" held daily. Immediately after supper, the next exercise was for each of the grown up children to produce their Rosaries and the entire family said the Rosary prayers together.

Oftentimes, my dad or mom told some short story of the pioneering days of the religious missionaries from Ireland who first evangelized our areas. Other times, one of my elder brothers or sisters or even a cousin or uncle told some story from the "lives of the Saints or from the Bible." Our parents and older siblings used folklore or epic stories to drive some Christian virtues home to us. All these folklore and pious and moral stories helped to motivate us to aspire to Christian virtues and practice socially accepted norms. They helped to mould our character, instilling real dread and hatred for evil and love of virtues. We were all "in quest of inner beauty" from that tender age.

Rather than engaging in unhealthy quarrels, rivalry, and troublesome behaviors that often characterize large families like ours, we were competing in showing charity, honesty, patience, industriousness, purity, and modesty, even at an early age. Compare this effect of traditions and prayers in family life to some of today's families where parents hardly pray with their children who are always busy with violent video games, shameful films, and sensual media programs! Just as the computers can only give you what you feed into them, so with the minds and hearts of growing teens and, in fact, any person of any age at all. Our minds reproduce the impressions that they are exposed to always, for good or for evil.

Rituals

Rituals in Igbo family life are ways of behavior that have so endured in a family and among a group, that often, nobody in living memory is able to explain their origin. Often, some parents or great elders in the family or village would say: "these rituals and traditions have been there before our forefathers, they originated with our earlier ancestors."

Rituals take various forms and could therefore, include gestures, signs, words, and substances or materials that accompany them. They have certain specifications and precision, with certain aurora of myth that surround their performance in a given culture. These rituals help us to pause and to reflect on the deeper meaning of the otherwise hurried daily lives that we live. Rituals among the Igbos have a unique and inexplicable way of lifting us into the realm of the divine, and placing us at the very threshold of the sacred.

For example, the invocation of God and of the ancestors, as a baby is being dedicated to God as its origin and maker during the child's naming ceremony in Igbo culture, ushers in such an awful silence and peace, revealing a tremendous mystery to all present. Every day, every hour, every moment; in the daily village life of the Igbo culture, rituals and ceremonies are being celebrated in small and in big ways— to sanctify time as a succession of life events. By means of rituals, in somewhat subtle ways, humans are in full communication with God and the spiritual realms daily.

Family rituals include the blessing of meals by the father or mother of the family or any of the elders that may be around during a family meal. Sometimes, however, a parent or elder may give one of the children, even the youngest, the opportunity to say the blessing before or after the meal. In like manner, a father or mother may bless the family members with holy water after morning or evening prayers. There are rituals in remembrance of the dead. In such ceremonies, special meals are cooked, particular clothes worn, and members present and absent, alive or dead are often mentioned in the intercessions. Folk songs, epic dances, or visits to particular sights often go with these celebrations.

It is the quiet reflection on the actions performed or words used that reveal more clearly the hidden meaning of these rites. Rituals are the surest ways of growing in spirituality and of reclaiming the spiritual values of a culture. It was with a deep understanding of the place of rituals in our human spiritual growth and psychological well being that an author wrote: "Rituals transform the state of powerlessness to one of effectiveness. Its prescribed form and predictability are part of its power to give shape to joy, form to grief, and order to the assertion of might and in so doing, contain and relieve our anxieties." [8] (La Farge 1982).

Passages

Numerous passages mark the lives of people in the Igbo culture, from the cradle to the grave. The various events of the year, the climatic seasons, planting and other farming seasons, holidays and holy days, births, deaths, and marriage engagements are all ritualized and solemnly celebrated in this culture. Even on a daily basis, people's goings and comings, work engagements and rests, meals, and various human encounters, all are ritualized.

In the Igbo family life, all these rites and passages are indeed the primordial forms of therapy that have been with this culture, all through their history. "These passages are golden opportunities for family members to open up to one another. People respond much more easily during these events because of the reverence accorded such occasions. Such reverence of course stem from the belief in the special and unique presence of the ancestral spirits and of the grace of God, on such occasions" (Great Elder, Edward Uformadu 1988).

Lastly, rituals are so vital because such occasions disrupt people's daily life routine and make them somehow amenable to change, to compromise, dialogue, and reconciliation. Such occasions are classified as sacred times, and so, Christian families seize such opportunities to allow God's grace to flow through their lives by including the celebration of prayer and the sacraments in these rituals.

A Family Ritual

In this family ritual, Fr. Greg is receiving his parent's blessing at home before leaving for his priestly ordination ceremony. Never you underestimate the power of parent's prayers and blessings. Their curse or abuses can equally have transgenerational, devastating consequences on their posterity.

Reconciliation Rituals And Conflict Resolutions
ORIKO (Eating together—communion)

In Igbo families as well as in the community, people have simple native approaches to reconciliation of family or clan members who are quarreling or fighting. For instance, it sometimes happens that a husband and wife have got into disagreements, had quarrels or even fights that have culminated in their not being able to talk with each other or even eat together anymore. When friends or relations of the parties happen to know of it, they set up elders in a quiet family meeting to look into the matter.

After the issues have been resolved, a day is set for the final reconciliation rite, which would in a way serve as a form of oath, to guarantee their safety, fidelity, and cooperation in the future. On the agreed date, the wife and mother of the family would cook a sumptuous meal, which will be eaten by all present at the ceremony. The husband and wife would eat from the same dish, as they had often done in the past, to demonstrate their unity in love, willingness to live in harmony in the future, all this, in the presence of their family and community members. It is like a renewal of their marriage commitments.

This meal called: Igba Oriko (eating together) is a form of oath taking. If a partner is conceited and goes against the promise that he or she had made to the spouse, to the community, and to God and the spiritual realm, it is believed that the defaulter would go sick, crazy, or die after eating the meal, which is the material that seals the oath taken. Therefore all who eat this meal, do so to their health and nourishment or otherwise to their own self destruction and condemnation. In this example, if a partner is sure not to keep the oath or the terms of settlement, he or she would not eat the meal so as not to poison himself or herself. We can see here that this ritual is based on the operation of that "moral law within," the conscience which we treated earlier in chapter one of this book.

Now, compare this Igba-Oriko (common meal) or Igba ndu (binding of lives or life-insurance) ritual, with St. Paul's warning about the Christian Eucharist in his first letter to the Corinthians two thousand years ago: "Whoever, therefore, eats the bread or drinks the cup of the Lord in an unworthy manner, will be answerable for the body and blood of the Lord. Examine yourselves, only then should you eat of the body and drink of the cup. For all who eat and drink without discerning the body, eat and drink judgment against themselves. For this reason, many of you are weak and ill, and some have died" (I Corinthians 11:27-30).

The Ritual Of Igba Ndu (Life Insurance Binding Of Lives)

As it is with a family, so it could also be for communities or other individuals in the community. If people are suspicious of one another, if a person feels that his or her life is in danger from another or others, the parties concerned would meet. After the settlement or oath, a meal or drink of some sort is taken to guarantee the safety of people's life. This is called Igba ndu (Binding of Life or life-insurance). It needs to be explained here that the term Igba ndu or life insurance does not connote the same meaning here in this Igbo cultural ritual as it is in our English usage of a person taking a life insurance premium. It is rather, a guarantee of safety, of the lives of those who have been through this ritual and oath so that justice may take its course. In a much deeper sense, it implies the binding together of the lives of all participants in mutual trust.

The ritual has two parts, which we may call matter and form. The words of enactment and of the oath taken is the form; while the material used whether it be food, drink, or any object, like when one has to swear on a shrine or Bible, is the matter of the ritual ceremony.

Summary

Both traditions and rituals are ways of behavior practiced by families and groups, and can be simple or complex in form. Telling a child short stories, singing some folk songs, and blessing the child before putting him or her to bed is a simple ritual and a tradition, which parents or elder siblings could maintain in their families.

I never left home on a journey, went in for an examination or embarked on any venture without first going down to my parents to ask for their blessing. Family traditions make us vividly aware of the hidden meanings and wealth of values that reside in various life events, which we could otherwise take for granted and so, lose their spiritual, social, moral, and psychological values. Traditions, rituals, and prayers effect healing, reconciliation, spiritual growth, peace, and unity among people who celebrate or observe them.

Among the Igbos, various events and passages of life are celebrated and ritualized and thus, they become traditions in given families and groups. These include: pregnancy, birth of a child, the naming ceremony of a child, the weaning and teething of a child, and so on. As some psychologists have rightly pointed out, people are most open to change, to reconciliation and growth at such events.

Rituals and traditions are solemn occasions believed to be richly suffused with God's graces and the blessings of ancestors who are normally invoked in these rites. The admirable cohesion and bonding that exists among the members of the Igbo cultural families has its roots in their rituals, traditions, and spirituality. These are among the factors that help to unite Igbo cultural families inseparably for life.

Chapter Three

Children's Upbringing In The Igbo-African Traditional Society And Culture

"If the children of a given generation are morally and properly educated and disciplined, there will be progress, order, happiness, and peace in the society, if they too, are able to give the same training to their posterity."
(Chief Rex Apofure, Kings' College 1966)

The Igbo-African Rites Of Passage

A. The Training Of The Igbo-Child, Begins At Pregnancy

It would be right to state that the training of the Igbo-African child in the Igbo-culture, begins right from the time of pregnancy of the unborn baby. This is true in the sense that the Igbos believe that a baby, once conceived duely in the womb, begins to respond to the rhythm and situations of the mother's life. For this reason, the mother must be helped to live out her life during this whole period of pregnancy in a way that will best promote the physical, mental, emotional, and psychological well-being of the baby as it develops in the womb.

"The Igbo-society that is expecting a new member," said my informant, "has their own expectations of what the child should be. The society wants truly healthy children who will lead her to greater heights of progress in the future. We don't want lazy, timid imbeciles. We value children, in great numbers but not just any type." (Anyi anaghi eji aku azu anu - ohia) We don't waste our wealth and resources in training beasts. (Anyalechi Njoku 1984)

B. The Pre-natal Stage

As an educational period for both mother and child, the pregnancy period has its own regulations in the Igbo-society. The expectant mother has a special diet that would enhance the healthy growth of the unborn baby as well as her own health. Therefore, she does not take alcohol, nor does she smoke or take herbs that could harm her baby. She exercises her body daily by carrying on her usual domestic chores as well as her economic activities but with great caution.

"An unbroken activity where possible, till the day of child-labor for the expectant mother, is believed to ensure an easy delivery and a strong healthy child. Idleness in the months of pregnancy without a good exercise is believed to lead to a difficult labor, a weak and lousy child. Above all, the expectant mother in Igbo-society is encouraged to participate in Women's dancings occuring in her neighborhood even on daily basis. She is to engage in a lot of humorous past-times such as singing, dancing, and all such joyful exercises. Other women in the community would do anything to delight the pregnant women to engage them in laughing exercises. They hold that laughter is a wholesome exercise for both mother and her unborn baby" (Mrs. Anastasia Opara 1986).

C. Birth

The newborn is welcomed with great joy and is at every step treated with a loving acceptance. Such loving acceptance is affirmed for instance, in the words of greeting which the dancing women who come at the announcement of the birth of a child in a village use: "Welcome our beloved child. Be sure, we will love you in our community and world, more than you have been loved in the womb and in the world you are coming from."

Then, would resound their clarion-call at child birth: onye muta, onye muta, ihe eji nwa eme buru ibu – o. eh, eh, eh, eh, eh, eh, eh, eh (sang three times in descending modulation). Obu gini-ee? Obu nwa-o.

This Igbo-chorus simply states: "Let all give birth, for we need innumerable children for innumerable ends and purposes." The unconditional love that the child receives would guarantee the child's trust for the parents and the community. All the children of the community would visit the new baby to play with him or her. Elders endeavor to come daily to see the baby and they all shower their blessings on the child as they fondle him or her. A new child is the center of attraction in the village, the talk of the town, especially among children and the elderly.

The nursing mother is never lonely, for there are always people of the community who would visit daily to see her and her baby. She receives presents of food, clothing, and all other items from people who come to rejoice with her. You can always know a family that has a new baby from the incessant echo of songs, of clapping, excitement and jubilation ringing from that compound every day for the first three months of the child's birth. A common rhythm that one would hear in this blessed compound several times each day as people come and go from that home runs thus: Onye ihe ọma di nmma bia gburu 'm aka (3 times) otu a mma nmma – eh, eh, otu a mma nmma, eh, eh (3 times). Whoever takes delight in goodness, let that person come and rejoice with us (3 times). This event is beautiful, yes, it is wonderful, yes, it is marvelous! Naturally, everybody wishes the best in his or her life. And since the Igbos hold that both goodness as well as evil are infectious, people would duely identify with a home and compound that is celebrating God's goodness and favors, that they too may be favored.

"It is believed too that instinctively, the new baby knows by the love and favors showered on him or her at every moment that he or she is dearly valued and appreciated. Again in this culture, one rarely visits a new baby with empty hands, but always with gifts. This is a gesture of thanksgiving and appreciation to God and a sign of solidarity of community members, and it is for the child's "wholesome health." According to the Igbos, the child is made to feel and believe that he or she has many people who love him or her and whom to love in return" (Mathilda Njokuocha 1985).

D. The Community Must Claim Their Child

As the baby continues to smile at the many faces that come up each day to greet him or her, one can overhear the comments of the elders who watch this most beautiful scenario: "Oh, see how he/she smiles at each and every new face that comes. The baby knows that he or she is loved, accepted and appreciated." These elders keep reassuring the baby: "We love you, we love you," and everyone who visits repeat the same. Igbo elders speak to the baby in these words and they firmly believe that the baby hears them but being yet unable to speak, responds in smiles and laughter.

Asked why the people besiege the new born baby in these first twelve to eighteen months with visits and presents much more than in the days ahead, the matron of the children's age group said: "We do not take it for granted that the child has come into our community and all is okay. We do everything possible to assure the child of our love, our care and acceptance of him or her as a community." The child is believed to be still more of a spirit than human and needs to have sufficient love and care to encourage him or her to remain in human society. As a community, the foundation of our relationship with the child must be strongly layed in the first year or the second and third years. This guarantees a healthy and strong personality (Madam Magdalene Uwakwe 1978).

Infancy Periods

The Naming Ceremony and After

In the Igbo family, the moment a child is born, the father of the child consults his own father or father-figure who gives the first name of the child. A date for the naming ceremony is then fixed for the third or fifth week to make sure that the child is not too tender for the strenuous ceremony and its rites. Before this ceremony, the child is first circumcised as the Igbo custom demands. Circumcision is one of those rituals that the Igbos and the Jewish people share in common.

The relations of the child as well as the village community are invited to the naming ceremony of the child, which takes place as early as 5 or 6 a.m. At the ceremony, several items are presented to the baby. After the grandparents and parents of the baby have given names to the baby, other elderly relatives like uncles and aunts also give names to the child. The items presented to the baby have their symbolic meanings in the culture of the Igbos. These include farming implements such as: cutlas or hoe. Also, seed crops like yam, coco yam and vegetable seeds which are native to the area are included. Other items like cooking oil, honey, alligator pepper and educational materials like pen or pencil are also presented. Many food items like wine, cereals and other edibles are among the dozens of items that are brought out at this event. The main occupation of an area determines what implements and items are presented to the child. A fishing village for instance would include lines and fish hooks among the items.

The child's grandfathers or grandmothers are present to carry the child on their laps as the items are being presented. For instance, the leader of the ceremony calling the child by some of his or her many names, dips a finger in the honey, touches the lips of the baby saying: ". . . taste this honey and know that life can be sweet at times but not always . . ." Or again, the leader putting the pen or pencil in the child's hand would say: "May you be anxious to learn and may God grant you the intelligence to excel in all you learn . . ." All present at the ceremony would answer "Amen" to these invocations. Since there are packets of such items like pen or pencil, all such materials are shared out to the attendants at the ceremony with the cooked food and drinks prepared for the event.

Most of the elders who attend the ceremony especially the members of the child's extended family circle, have names for the child. Names are given according to family history of the named, according to the events surrounding their lives and so forth. Igbo names are symbolically important in the culture. Such names include:

(a) Ikechukwu (God's power)
(b) Chukwuma (God knows what we don't know)
(c) Chinyere (God's gift)
(d) Ogechi (God's time is the best)
(e) Ozoemena (May misfortune not befall us again)

This naming ceremony by the adults is concluded sharply for the attendants to get into other activities of the day.

Prayers and blessings continue to pour from the lips of all attendants till they all disperse after blessing the mother and child and the father of the house. The final prayer by the group attending, calls God's blessings on the entire extended family of the new baby. They also invoke the ancestors and spirits who govern the village, to protect and bless the child who is seen as the youngest and dearest member of the village community.

The Children's Naming Ceremony And Party (Igba Miri Ofe, Soup-Ritual)

The "Soup-Evening" as it is popularly called by the children, takes place by the evening of the adults' naming ceremony for the new baby or on some other day within the same week. The event is both the children's party and a ceremony ushering in the newborn baby into the world of the children of the village. It is a most joyful celebration for the children of a given village and includes children and adolescents alike.

It is usually held in the evening and is an open-air-celebration; open to nature's beauties, with the moonlight and all other celestial luminaries witnessing as the children jubilantly sing and dance far into the night. The ceremony is directed by the children's matrons and patrons who also direct their age groups. These leaders are to see that the ceremony is conducted peacefully and the rituals followed in their rightful order. The new baby is presented to the children's group amid great applause, singing, and dancing. They are given the child's names and they repeat the names three times and congratulate the parents of the baby.

Most of them, especially the younger ones endeavor to carry the baby briefly, hug the baby or shake its tiny hands. Tins of baby powder used for the child are brought out for the children to use. Each of these children must as a rule, rub some of the powder on his or her cheeks as a ritual and mark of sharing in the child's life and as a symbol of solidarity among the children of the village. All types of food, grains, cereals, vegetables, salad and above all the popular soup prepared with stockfish and crayfish, are shared.

From the children's voices ringing through the still air, the entire village is able to know that such a ceremony was taking place. This formally, is the beginning of the solidarity and bonding that now exists between the new baby and the rest of the children of the village or clan. In this ceremony, some elders, men and women, are present to give brief moral instruction to the children. The learning of folklores, riddles, and native songs also take place. It is a most exciting celebration that children look forward to, because of the rich display of traditional rituals, moral lessons, epic songs and dances which are learned. This event is an induction ceremony which reaffirms in the participants, a sense of belonging to their particular kinship, as a group.

The community-spirit that characterize most adult behavior patterns in Igbo-society as we have seen in Chapter Two, is in fact inculcated into children right from infancy in ceremonies like "a baby's naming ceremony". These body of knowledge of approved human behavior in the Igbo-society, is made to take root in the child as he or she goes through rites of passage of human development from infancy to adulthood. Therefore, at every naming ceremony, elders come forward to re-emphasize certain cultural values, the do's and don'ts. Thus, in one of these events that I attended, a woman elder and matron of the children's age group addressed them as follows: "My children, let these be imprinted in your hearts and minds, that our Igbo customs and traditions do not tolerate or condone misbehaviors in children nor in adults. You must show unalloyed respect, loyalty, and love, to your parents, elders, teachers, and in fact all lawfully constituted authorities. You must be duty-conscious, performing your allotted tasks at home, in school and in the society. Our culture does in fact, punish laziness. You must be humble, honest, and courageous to be able to take your rightful places in your families, in the school, and the community. Stealing, falsehood, cheating, fighting, impurity of any form, should not be seen in your lives. Therefore, you must be true children of your beloved parents and worthy sons and daughters of our noble village" (Madam Philomena Ihuoma Njokuocha 1988)

On another occasion of children's village festival at which I was present, a certain elder and patron of one of the boys age group came forward to admonish the group, and he said: "Children, beware as you go through your life stages, to do nothing that you or your parents will regret. Therefore, be sure that you do nothing that will soil your family's reputation and bring down God's wrath on this village. If you do, people will put the blame on your parents and on this community. You will suffer for it physically but the ripples will spread grimly on.

Our culture and traditions still hold that:

(a) Ihe nwa ewu na ebe, nne ya mara ya (It is the mother goat that taught the baby goat to cry incessantly the way it does). That your behaviors are inherited or learned from your parents.

(b) Ihe egbe muru ahapughi ibu okuko (That whatever is born of a kite or hawk would naturally prey on the young chicken).

And indeed, the Igbos see these axioms as natural truths and therefore they say that Obara anaghi atu asi (Blood does not tell lies). That is, behaviors are genetical (Nicholas Obasi 1980).

The adolescents in the children's ceremony of this nature are able to understand these types of moral lessons and axioms and they endeavor to preserve their knowledge of them by memorizing them and discussing them and asking questions from their parents, their uncles and aunts. Those of them who prove themselves wise in the knowledge of these customary norms often become group leaders in their age groups and would be future patrons and matrons as adults. In general, such moral lessons serve great needs in helping to form the character of these youths in the community. Issues raised in village gatherings are discussed in family and kinship meetings. Children confront their parents with such issues that they do not understand during and after meals. Such issues whether they are moral, religious, spiritual, political, economic, or historical, are the type of discussions that children excel in, during their years of upbringing in the village community. Thus, they are well formed characters by the time they get into their young adulthood.

Though, the Igbos have not done much to document their traditional education, this oral tradition as shown above has been quite effective from generation to generation. Unfortunately, these traditional values are fast disappearing even in Igbo land, since the family and community settings of the past are no more. A new way of effecting this type of training in children stands as a challenge to people of all cultures round the world today.

The Formal Training Of A Child In The Igbo-African Rites Of Passage

Aims Of This Training

The Igbo-African rites of passage has the following goals in view:

From the very conception of a child, the Igbo community aims at preparing the child (if I may use the analogy of the American game of football), "to be able to receive the ball from the father and mother; and guided and supported by his or her family and community in the training they give him or her, to move from the quarterback and maneuver through all the lines of defence, till he or she is able to make a touchdown" (Charles Ogugua 2000).

This Is What The Attainment Of Maturity Is Like In The Igbo-Society

Since every individual Igbo is a community of all that make up his or her relationships in life, the game of life cannot be played in isolation, but always in the community of relationships. No one can therefore, receive the ball from parents and score it all alone, but always as a member of a team. If an individual family member fails to play his or her position well, the team would become porous, dysfunctional and the game would be lost. Whether this is caused by parents or a child in the family, the result is disaster for the family. If a family is stigmatized, the community is in debt. If the community is in crisis. The whole society or state is in disarray.

It is because of this interrelatedness of people and their interdependence in the community that the Igbos would pose the question which is: Onye gbakere oria nwa ya nwua, ogbakela? (If one should recover from a sickness and his or her child then dies from the same sickness, did the person really recover?) For the Igbos, the answer is no! They therefore assert that when one eye is wounded and cries, that the second eye also shades tears in response. It would be most unnatural for it to be otherwise. In practical life situations in today's society, many people are inconsiderate of others. No feelings for their neighbors, all because of the individualism and selfishness that rule our societies.

The Igbo-African rites of passage which is the foundation of the upbringing of children in the Igbo culture, prepares the Igbo child to take his or her place in the community and flourish with the other members, for the greater good of his or her family, of the community and of society at large. Because the Igbo culture would not want any dsyfunctioning in a family or the community, the culture and its tradition prepares the child not to contribute to such a unhappy state of affair. Therefore, the Igbos insist saying: Onye na egbo ǫgu gbo nra (Whoever wants to prevent a fight, should endeavor to stop insinuators or instigators).

Both individuals, the family and the community must cooperate in the training of the Igbo child. The environment of the child's life which is the community, must be such that the child has only healthy influences that will promote the training that he or she receives. The Igbo systemic life is based on prevention rather than intervention. The whole system is one long therapeutic process that goes on imperceptibly in the primordial rituals and celebrations that I have been describing throughout this book.

The Many Dimensions Of The Igbo Rites Of Passage

The training and upbringing of a child in the Igbo-African rites of passage has so many dimensions. These include: historical, social, spiritual, religious, moral, cultural, educational, economic, political, and psychological dimensions of their lives. These dimensions are never treated distinctively as such, but always coalesce with one another in the system of life that exits in this culture. A family could have a child who has attained the physical years, but not the standard maturity encompassing at least a modicum of all the above dimensions. Where this happens, the family would have failed the community in their son or daughter.

It is the training that the child receives during this passage or transition from childhood to young adulthood that the child would live out in the community, the society and world for the rest of his or her life. "We make the world," says James Brown. If the community releases a harmonious note of a human character into the society, the society will resound with melody! If the society lets out a hundred sour notes of human beings into the world, because time is irreversible, those discordant notes of humans will infect the society adversely.

The result would be that the entire universe of creation would feel this disharmony in the apathy, strife, violence,

immorality, injustice, and brutality which those sad note.
would wreck in their trail round the world from one
generation to another. It is for this reason that the Igbos say:
Madu bu njo ala and conversely, Madu bu mma ala (Humans
make the society either good or bad).

1. Religious Dimension

As has been so aptly described by early
anthropologists and missionaries to Nigeria, the Igbos
are deeply religious people who are known to "eat,
dress, work, and walk religiously." As a rule, parents
and the society do everything to inculcate this
religious spirit in their children even from infancy.
Thus, when a family is having their night prayer, the
mother of the family would put a rosary on the neck
of her baby and try to involve him or her in the
family prayer atmosphere.   Consistently,   children
are taken to all the prayer meetings in the village
squares, to Sunday Services and Masses, and other
religious activities. In the beginning, these prayer
meetings and Liturgical Services serve more like
socialization programs for the younger children with
their friends that they meet in the gatherings. As they
grow older, they start to imbibe the piety and other
ends and purposes of prayer that adults enjoy. In this
way, the children develop personal interest in the
religion of their parents and would be the ones to
remind their parents of the time for family evening,
or morning prayers, and the Sunday Services.

Igbo parents in fact, use religion and spirituality to help them train their children in discipline and responsibility, in honesty and industry so that these children do not cause problems in the family. As I had earlier stated in Chapter One, Igbo children are brought up with the same religious, spiritual, and moral principles that their parents and elders practice.

2. Spiritual Dimension

The Igbos believe that "a person's primary goal in life is to know what purpose one's creator has willed for him or her and to order one's life accordingly." Spirituality and religion are therefore among the major weapons by which parents and the community mould the character of children, in the family and society. When children begin their journey of learning with religion and spirituality, they very easily become amenable to the training they receive in the years of their passage into adulthood. Being spiritually immunized, children are more loyal and cooperative with parents, their elders and teachers. Right from infancy, children are trained to have very strong awareness of God's abiding presence and are schooled to know the function of their guardian spirits and their ancestors. They are made to know and believe that they can win God's blessings and the favor of the divine spirits, if they comport themselves becomingly well in life. Parents and the community seize every opportunity to impart these religious and spiritual values to children, knowing that on these values depend the efficacy of the training given to children in their years of passage into adulthood.

3. Social And Cultural Dimensions

On the social and cultural levels, the children are made to learn and understand the skills of interpersonal relationships in the family and society in general, and in the married life in particular. Therefore, from the age of nine or ten for both boys and girls, they are inducted into the community life obligations, privileges and rights. From this age, the children are readily seen sweeping their family compounds in the morning. They sweep the village and market roads during the weekends especially on the big market days. The children also learn about the sacred festivals: the traditional celebrations of the village Christmas (Igba egwu) the new yam festival (iri ji ofuu) of marriage engagement (Igba nkwu nwanyi) the age grade ceremony (ime ebiri) and the ceremony of clothing to end the pubertal rites (iwa akwa).

In the children's age grades, they organize group labor programs to help in cleaning the compounds and farms of widows and the poorer members of the community. They join the adults in various community projects. All these are geared towards their training in maturity whether they fulfill social, economic or political ends. For recreation and socialization, these children gather in some evenings for what is called Egwu-Ọnwa (Moon-light plays). The children do this separately according to their different sexes but in the same village square. Such activities provided the opportunity for the needed interactions between the boys and the girls. They are invariably supervised by their adult patrons and matrons. It is through such interactions between boys and girls of given villages that the children could learn healthy bisexual relationships. It is also through such interactions that some of them are able to choose their marriage partners for the future.

The Igbo culture is however very strict in supervising this interaction between the two sexes. The culture does not allow boys and girls to relate too closely in any setting. This is done to forestall any promiscuous behavior and the teenage pregnancy which is of course a taboo in the Igbo culture. To explain this measure in the relationship of the sexes, one of my formators in the seminary said: "...the opposite sexes do not interact loosely in our culture because the hawk and the young chicken do not go to the same market. The cat and the rat do not enter any form of partnership. Fuel and the naked fire do not form a coalition government" (Monsignor Michael Eneja 1974).

Igbo Children's Dancing Group

Igbo-African children in Miami, Florida, U.S.A., on stage, learning their cultural dance. The youngest kid in this picture was then two years of age. African children imbibed their culture from infancy as the most effective way of transmitting VALUES.

4. Social Dimension

Children in the Igbo culture are not only taught the geography and economy of their land but are diligently trained in various fields of human endeavor available in the society. Parents, the age grades, the community, the schools and society at large, each has a role in teaching and training the Igbo child in some aspect of the general economy of the land and of preparing the child for his or her life profession.

As a rule, a young man never talks of marriage in the Igbo culture until he has trained out in a profession that can guarantee a steady salary that can maintain his new family. Moreover, he should be able to point to his own personal house where to welcome his bride and new family. Likewise, a young lady does not enter marriage until she has acquired a reasonable profession and skill that can sustain her and her children in the new family that she is starting, in case some misfortune should befall her husband in his own career.

In general, people do not jump into the marriage and the married life in the Igbo-society till they are prepared socially, economically, educationally, and so forth on the life. "Marriage is for mature adults, not for children," the Igbos would say. Even in the old system, where children were betrothed in marriage by their parents, the partners never joined themselves to live the married life, until they were fully prepared as mature adults for the family life. Such early engagements only helped to prepare them well enough, so that as my father said: "The two families could become relatives before they can become brothers and sisters in love."

5. Education

In the traditional Igbo-society, a conscious effort was made to instruct and discipline the youngsters and prepare them for life's challenges. From the age of nine or ten in both boys and girls, children were given sound instructions, and acquired knowledge in various work fields. Literary arts, agricultural skills, crafts, music, and dances. For a select few who have the potentials, there is training in physical strength and agility for selection of wrestlers and warriors, athletes and acrobats.

In general, all children are trained from this tender age to discipline all their faculties so as to bring out their best human qualities. These trainings are intensified in their pubertal rites and initiations till they attain their adulthood. From the dawn of human history, indigenous and informal education had taken variety of forms in various parts of Africa. It was mostly non-literate in nature. Only the Vai of Liberia and the Mum of Cameron had invented their own system of writing; no other African group did.

Informal education among the Igbos of old was more of children imitating what the adults did and through apprenticeship, they perfected them in specific fields. A girl was in the old system merely trained by her mother to be an ideal housewife and mother of a family. She was trained in the community in petites trades, gardening, and cooking. For a boy, he learned his father's trade, art or craft as well as those of some uncles of his. In addition, he learned the prevailing general patterns of hunting, drumming and basic farming skills.

6. Historical Dimension

From their earliest years, children are taught the history and origins of their villages and clans. Through folklores, epics and drama, they learn about their great ancestors and heroes of their villages and clans. They are taught histories of great events of the past in various spheres of life. The comprehensive knowledge of these histories formed materials for reviews and tests in various village, clan and family celebrations for the children.

These folklores, plays and proverbs are passed on orally from one generation to another. Unfortunately, oral traditions are among those things that the media saturated countries of today cannot fully appreciate.

The Age Group System In Igbo-Society

The place of the youths in traditional Igbo-society is primary. The youths are always referred to as "the greater tomorrow." Explaining this point, a great elder and community leader said: "No one ever prays to be greater than his or her child, rather, every one prays that his or her child may be greater than him or her. It is the mark of a civilized society to make progress. Therefore we always pray and hope for a greater and better tomorrow" (H. R. H.; Eze Edmund Osuagwu 1992)

In his book, "Environment and Politics In West-Africa," R. J. Harrison Church (1963) said: "African children get into their cultures early, and there are no abrupt shifts." [1] This statement is indeed very true of Igbo children. Generally, children copy what they see their elders doing. In the Igbo community, the age group system is used to order the classes of human beings according to their ages in most social affairs. The age grades range from the youngest which may be the ten year old among boys and the twelve year old among girls, to the centenarians, which is the oldest group among both men and women.

1. The Boys Age Grade

The boys in their age group organize group activities like games and sports competitions, between one village and another. They also organize hunting expeditions and farming projects in which they often help to cultivate or harvest the farms of old or widowed members of the community. They help to mend the village roads, clean the village markets and carry out other activities as their civic duties.

Above all, the age groups have a very powerful Constitution with laws and regulations to govern their Union. If a boy is unruly or disloyal to his parents, once the report reaches any of the boys' age group members, the Union penalizes the boy seriously. He is made to apologize to his parents, promise loyalty and love to them, and do the manual labor imposed on him by the Union. "An organization or group, is greater and stronger than an individual member." The Igbos would say: Ofu onye anaghi esiri oha nri (One person does not cook for a community, meaning that an individual cannot challenge a community to a duel). By such disciplinary measures, the age group members are trained to be law abiding and well behaved, both in their families, in the school, and in the society.

A Youth Group At Manual Labor

I, at work with a youth group in the Parish-Farm. You can best teach them by example. If you don't model what you teach, you're teaching something else and the children will be confused.

2. The Girls' Age Grade

The girls' age group has the same organization as the boys and carry out various corporal works of mercy among the sick, the poor and the aged in the community. They organize dances, plays, arts and craft that would be relevant to their roles as future mothers and housewives. Their constitution does not spare defaulters. If a girl is guilty of any act of disobedience to parents or proved indecent or immoral in any way, she is often made to do public penance and render apology to her parents and may be suspended for some time. In this way, girls grew into responsible ladies that would in future make exemplary mothers and wives and mentors to the young. They always have a good adult woman as their matron and guide.

It is necessary to note that in Igbo traditional culture and society, the group activities of males and females are clearly defined, each in its own place, time and mode. The males and females rarely have joint activities. If they do, they always stay separately for reasons already explained in the Igbo axioms on the different sexes. This tradition of "male-female distance," is taught almost from infancy in various ways. This had helped the Igbos to maintain their moral standards with regard to sexual behaviors. For the same reason, men and women have remained faithful in their marriages.

The new trend of uni-sex fashions in clothing, dances and other interactions is however frowned at in the villages of Igbo land. In effect, sexual misconduct is very much on the increase in the cities and towns of Igbo land where these measures are not being observed, nor the age group system maintained.

Moral Education And Disciplinary Formation Of Children In the Igbo-Traditional Society And How This Approach Can Aid Counseling Today

Africans in general believe strongly that the true worth of a person is seen in his or her behavior. Thus, the Igbos of South-Eastern Nigeria have an axiom which says: Agwa bu nmma (Manner maketh a man). A morally well behaved person is valued above all riches, learning, power, etc. Every society has its customs and values and therefore, people are said to be well behaved when they conduct themselves according to the accepted norms and values of their society. When however, people behave in ways contrary to these norms, they are said to be immoral. The society or group is ordered, peaceful, and progressive if its people behave morally well.

Stages Of Character Formation In Igbo Children

Stage One:
Dependence On Outside Authorities – Children Live and Act On The Authority And Guidance Of Others

It is precisely at this stage that the formation of character in Igbo children begins but with cautious, relaxed and firm stance. From the age of five, children in this culture are already aware of their gender. Girls prefer to move with their own sex and boys with theirs. Parents, elder siblings and the family elders continue to remind the growing child in words like: "go and play with fellow boys and not girls. Don't sit like a boy or climb trees as they do, you are a girl. You must be gentle with girls and don't push them roughly as you would do with fellow boys."

At this time too, between the ages of five and ten, the girls are encouraged to stay around their moms in the kitchen and to join in the house chores that are mainly for women but not strictly for them alone. Little boys stay more closely to their fathers and uncles who as elders are known for imparting the moral code and societal norms to youths. Growing children are taught to show respect to their immediate senior siblings, to parents and all elders, especially their teachers and other constituted authorities. Naturally, the Igbo traditional society at every level is very sensitive to issues of respect, misbehavior and good behavior. Everybody takes up the duty or obligation to make corrections, teach good behavior both in words and deed and punish and reprimand misbehavior. Any person could leash out a corrective measure at any time, anywhere, and to any child whether it be one's relative or not. This is because, as my uncle said: "...we are all molecules in the one river. If the molecules get dirty, the river is poisoned or infected and there is nowhere to move the entire river, to purify it, and everyone will suffer. Whatever gets dirty is carried to the river to clean or purify it. What happens if the river should become dirty; where do you carry it to?" (Moses Oleka 1977). What is implied here is that, it is the community that moulds and models human behavior as judge. If the community becomes corrupt, both community and members are lost.

The analogy here is very apt and clear: the community or society is the river. Each one of us is a molecule making up that body of water, the river. In the Igbo culture therefore, parents, elders and the community, take the moulding of the character of children at this stage of their life development seriously because the culture believes that lasting character traits are formed at this tender age in children. They compare a child at this stage to a tender plant. If you want to bend the plant away from a nearby building for instance, you either do it now or it would be too late later. After the stems have matured, bending it, would be a tug of war unless you want to destroy it. Therefore the Igbos would say that "One does not learn to use his or her left hand in old age" (Anaghi amu aka ekpe na nka).

In general, this stage when children can cram or memorize anything that they are taught, is believed to be the best time to teach them and direct them on the path you want them to follow in life. They ask questions and get clarifications as they grow.

Stage Two:
Self Dependence – Children Begin Gradually to Experiment With The Dictates Of Their Own Reason And Conscience

From the age of ten, boys join their age group Union while girls join theirs at about twelve. Even though they are inclined to follow their individual consciences, they usually seek the opinion of their peer group for validation. Parents and elders work more carefully with teens at this stage, to make sure they do not stray from the norms of the society, and from family values. Children realize for the first time that they can maintain their individual views different from those of parents, and others in the society. Parents and the society however put a restraint or check on this freedom. By nature, humans detest pain and seek all that is pleasurable.

Thus children at this stage of formation, are indoctrinated in a way. With vivid illustrations from epic stories, folklores and riddles, children are made to know that rewards follow good behavior while punishment and retribution, follow evil behaviors. When children go against traditional rules of conduct in the family, the schools or the society, they are slightly punished to reinforce what they had learned from the fables and riddles. Therefore, whether they are convinced or not, children at this stage do their best to be law abiding. This is done either to win favor or reward or to avoid punishment and the embarrassment that such brings on the individual in the midst of his or her age group members and peers.

Conforming To The Socially Approved Norms

The interrelatedness of people in the Igbo-society, makes it all the more difficult for any person to maintain a purely isolated and individualistic stance in life. Social interaction is the order of life in this culture and one's life is palatable only in conformity with societal norms. An individual therefore, has no choice than to swim with the current of the time in which he or she lives.

Stage Three:
Children Endeavor To Be In The Good Book Of Parents And Other Authorities

In their early teens, children in the Igbo culture are taught to be exemplary in their behavior. The Igbos like to quote cases of such exemplary children to encourage others to strive for goodness. Many incentives are used to encourage good behavior, while all forms of threat and mild punishment are used to discourage bad behavior.

There are such beliefs like: "A well behaved child brings countless blessing of God to his or her family. A person going to market meets with good luck and God's favors when a well behaved teen helps the person to lift his or her commodity on the way to market. Or again, if a well behaved child helps a planter to drop the seeds into the soil at the farm, the crops would germinate and grow very well." These may sound superstitious or weird to people who do not know about this culture but such belief system is part of the people's life and personality and a counselor can best understand them from their own background and world view. The simple message in this belief is that goodness attracts goodness. Therefore, it is good to be good.

Practical Lesson On Community-Spirit

The youngest age group in the Parish learning the community-spirit by laboring at the new church building site. Children learn character by direct imitation of adults not in theory. If it is not lived out, it doesn't register

Stage Four:
Children Are Helped To Maintain The Social Order

In this system, when a family, the community or village has deliberated on a matter, approved or ratified it, that matter becomes binding. It is ipso facto, seen as a decree not just of men alone but of heaven too. In essence, what the unanimous voice of the community has decreed is considered approved and blessed by God, the ancestors and the spirits who protect the community. A moral body or group in the Igbo culture is able to attain their objectives with the cooperation of the members because of the strong belief that the spiritual realm are also involved in the operations of a group. Due respect and cooperation therefore marks group practices. So, a child has to abide by the societal norms.

Stage Five:
Following The Rule Of Conscience

At this level of development in the growing child, the adolescent simply follows what his or her own conscience decides. This stage connotes a high level maturity in a person's moral development. At this point, one is not just striving for acceptance, competence, and recognition in the society, but for excellence and perfection. The individual is now "in quest of inner beauty."

To be recognized in the Igbo society as "a good person" (ezigbo madu) does not mean to be "a nice person" in a simple and general sense. It means to excel in virtuous qualities, being perhaps benevolent and merciful, considerate, patient and long-suffering, sympathetic, honest, philanthropic and truly loving. People are often referred to by such virtues.

Teen Friendship

It is good to consider at this point, interactions between the youngsters especially among the different sexes, in the Igbo culture. The Igbo traditional society of old, did not very much encourage friendship and interaction between teenage boys and girls. Sex was a taboo and sexual issues were hardly discussed openly both in the family life, the schools, and in the society. All about sex is left to the time of marriage and marriage was essentially for procreation.

Courtship was not elaborate save after the would-be partners have fulfilled the customary rites and prescriptions. The Igbo society feared the possibility of promiscuity, should teenagers be left to trifle with such vital issue as sex and intimacy. Above all, they dreaded possible teenage pregnancy and abortion all of which were abominable and a taboo in the culture. The Igbo parents and society of today however, do give room to interaction between teens of the opposite sexes but with much restrictions.

Peer Pressure Among The Youths

In this culture generally, teenagers who have been truly part of their family system and maintained their rightful places among their brothers and sisters have great security and self-esteem. The support they have from their siblings, parents, and the extended family system protect and prevent them from succumbing easily to peer pressures. Moreover, one's peer group in the Igbo-society are often members of one's age group or other age groups.

The age grade as a traditional institution in this system has strict rules and regulations that govern the life of its members. Each age group is mentored and monitored by a renowed elder who with the cabinet of officers governing the group, are able to keep track of members' lives and their association outside their families. Because of the age group influence on the lives of members, teenagers in Igbo cultural society are well protected from possible adverse impact that peer pressure often has on adolescents in general.

Morality, Religion And Discipline In Youths' Upbringing, Today

Under this chapter on the upbringing of children, it is necessary to consider together, the three elements of morality, religion, and discipline. This is because the three are contingently related. Each of them enriches, strengthens, and validates the others in the vital program of formation of character and education of children, all of which deal with human behavior. Furthermore, their operation always involve the following of rules by the free, uncoerced choices of rational human beings, in their relationship with others.

More and more, people today regret the loss of the sense of values in some of our present day youth and the need for moral revival. News prints, conventions, and seminars talk of moral decadence, indiscipline, and juvenile delinquency.

Factors Contributing To Indiscipline And Immorality In Youths Today

Certain factors have contributed to this unfortunate situation of things. Secularism has taken the place of religious education in schools. A major problem today is the capitalistic tendencies of many societies which eulogizes wealth and the wealthy no matter by what means the wealth has been acquired. The goal here is to get rich and get it quickly, the end justifies the means! Added to this menace is the care free attitude of some parents and teachers who have not been good models for their children at home and in the schools. Urbanization and the subsequent destruction of the old communities and families with the work situation that has made both parents full time workers. Little or no time is given to the care of children in most families today. In reality therefore, children are not the cause but only the victims of these circumstances in most cases.

No one should be surprised that children of today often behave differently from the way their parents and grandparents did in past decades. As Ron Brandt (1993) has rightly observed, "the factors that shape children's lives in today's society differ greatly from those of yesteryears. Also, because of social and economic changes, family patterns and work arrangements have irrevocably altered." Thus, many children today, receive less guidance from their parents. Fewer adults in the community make it their responsibility to know and to look out for children. Today, children learn about values and how to behave, mainly from television and from their peers." [2] Compare this with the Igbo community life upbringing of children earlier in this chapter.

Moral Training And Education In Children

What does it mean to be moral? One is moral when one's behavior is in line with the accepted norms and values of the society. When one's behavior falls short of the accepted norms and values of one's society, the person is said to be immoral. When we talk of morality, certain values and standards are already taken for granted. First of all, morality pre-supposes the existence of some person or persons who behaved in a certain way or is affected by the behavior of another, but never in-vacuo. It is against this background that one's action is being judged moral or immoral. Secondly, for an action to have merit or de-merit, it must exclude any type of force or coercion, but must be freely chosen. Thirdly, the use of reason and judgment, must guide the autonomous decision and action. Lastly, altruism or that self-effacing grace, which considers others' interests must be present in the actor—at least implicitly.

The Root Of Our Problem: The Disintegration Of Our Natural Families

As I pointed out in the last chapter, the family is the first school, the first church, the cradle of civilization. Traditionally, therefore, the family is the primary teacher and moral formator of a child. The failure of the family to fulfill this role for so many children in our time has created a moral vacuum. Sylvia Hewlett (1991) states that "American children, rich and poor alike, suffer a level of neglect that is unique among developed nations." Despite the decrease in the number of children per family, overall child well-being has declined." [3]

In "Dan Quayle Was Right" (April 1993), Barbara Dafoe Whitehead synthesizes the social science research on the decline of the two biological parent family in America: "If the current trends continue," she said, "less than half of the children born today, will live continually with their own mother and father throughout childhood . . . An increasing number of children will experience family breakup two or even three times during childhood. Children of most dysfunctional families are more likely to be poor, have emotional and behavioral problems, fail to achieve academically, get pregnant, abuse drugs and alcohol, get in trouble with the law and be sexually and physically abused than children of good functioning two parent families.

Family disruptions have been felt more by schools where children from dysfunctional homes act out aggressively. They are so upset and preoccupied with the escalating scenario of their dysfunctional families that they cannot concentrate in their class works." [4] Thus, family disintegration gives additional responsibility to school character formators.

Fourthly, the decision must be acted upon to be a complete operation and a moral act.

What is moral training? It is that kind of training given to persons with a view to making them behave in accordance with morally accepted rules within a group of people or a community. A local illustration would be this: Among the Igbos, children are taught by their parents to respect elders. In my home culture, younger children are taught, not to call their elders by their names. The younger calls the older Dee (Senior brother) or Ndaa (Senior sister) as the case may be. In greeting, children do not shake hands directly with their parents and elders. Rather, children could bow or lower their heads gently in greeting, or fold their hands respectfully. They could also shake their elders or parents' hands using both hands instead of one and at the same time lowering their heads respectfully. This is a gesture of reverence and humility on the part of the younger person and which in turn is believed to draw God's blessing on the younger.

Children are not to join in their parents or elders' discussion unless invited. In any gathering, elders take their seats before the younger ones. Women are of course given preference always. This type of moral training extends to the schools where the teachers assume the role of parents. Thus, the students respect their teachers in the same way they respect their parents. The younger students likewise respect their senior students as they do their senior brothers and sisters at home.

With regard to the moral training of children, while the Western or modern approach advocates that children volunteer to learn these values when they have attained a reasonable age, and anything of punishment be ruled out in the process, the Igbo-African system is of a different view.

"Research and experience shows that the most effective and lasting result in this moral training and education of children is attained when children step into it from infancy. Therefore, it hasn't got to be voluntary per se, since children at age five for instance cannot understand or judge for themselves, what is best for them. We can only say that it is partially or presumably voluntary" (Mrs. McIntyre Gray 2000).

Secondly, mild sanctions or punishments are intrinsic part of the training process for we must admit too that enduring a minor pain for a much higher, overall good of the trainee is better than an ineffective but painless approach. After all, training in athletics and games and in fact, any worthwhile field of endeavor, entails both physical and emotional pain often times. Some have criticized the tradition of giving children the moral rules and disciplinary regulations to recite and memorize. This is the first step, which is the best way to involve the children at their tender age and to get them interested even though they cannot yet understand what they are memorizing. The training continues with the frequent recitation and elucidation on the rules which they already have. As they grow older, their knowledge and understanding of these rules deepen and with the process of education, they are able to practice them meaningfully.

We need to remember that it is only the values that take root in our lives that we internalize. In effect, the goals we want the children to strive for, the values we want them to imbibe, must be practiced daily over a period of time till they become a habit or way of life. The children test themselves on the practice of these values, judge their performance on daily basis, and penalize or reward themselves as the case may be. When we teach children about honesty, truthfulness, and cleanliness for example, the children want to see these beautiful attitudes, demonstrated in concrete life situations and they will be encouraged to imitate or copy them. If parents or teachers teach one thing but do the opposite, they are teaching something else and the children will be less convinced if not confused. In the language of the Igbos, these children will see their teachers and parents as Soro okwum, esola omume' m' (follow my words but not my deeds), which of course is hypocrisy. In the Igbo-African upbringing of children, when the children in their pubertal program are taught team work and group cooperation for instance, the system in the community has been set to practice these values in their age group duties in their family life and in their community life engagements.

For me, a value that is not lived out, is still an embryo and in an age of partial birth abortion, its chances of survival is too infinitesimal to reckon with.

How Children Imbibe Their Moral Training

Naturally, children go through stages in their understanding and practice of moral rules as they are being trained in the family, in the school, and in the society. At the first stage, children obey rules, not necessarily out of conviction or to gain spiritual merit, but more out of fear, less the elders whether parents, teachers or senior brothers or sisters would punish them. At the second stage of their moral development, they see obedience to moral rules as bringing rewards and so, satisfying their own needs as well. They begin to associate the giving of gifts and praises from parents or others, with good behavior.

In yet a final stage, children come to believe that so long as they are faithful to moral rules, they would maintain good relationship with others. That they would win the approval of others especially peers and authorities whom they respect or fear. Since children at this stage also associate punishment with misbehavior, they want to be free of punishment and so do their best to behave in praiseworthy manner. This of course help to build up their self-esteem and mental health.

At this level of moral development in the children, if punishment and reward were to be removed, or if nobody would disapprove of their bad behavior, they would probably have behaved differently. They would follow the easier way out of things for humans, by nature prefer pleasure to pain, soft life to hard life. The implication in this case is that the moral values they have learned have not been internalized. These values can only be internalized if they are lived out over a long period, to augment and consolidate their moral training.

Punishment And Self Discipline In The Process Of Internalizing Moral Values In Children

The whole process of moral upbringing of children, should lead necessarily to self discipline or self control. We should not confuse being self disciplined, with being a disciplinarian, nor should we equate discipline with punishment. A disciplinarian may or may not be self disciplined. A disciplinarian depends on force and punishment to move people to obey rules and regulations. This of course connotes the idea of regimentation.

Under a disciplinarian, people do not follow the rules out of conviction necessarily. It all means that if the disciplinarian is away, the rules may not be obeyed. If the threats of punishment, force and canes are removed, the subjects may not live according to the laws. In this case, the subjects are not yet converted to order and discipline because conversion comes from conviction and faith in a value presented. It may take force to win, but it takes love to win over, which is conversion. Effecting discipline in people can best be done by winning them over to the values you teach and model.

Rather than put constraints on other's freedom, the teacher can use the love-techniques to get the subjects, put those constraints on their own freedom themselves once they are convinced of the greater good involved in the values. Thus, self discipline is best attained through conscientization in moral education. Religion and spirituality cannot be ruled out in the program of moral education and self discipline if it is not to remain a mere teaching on morals.

The education in many schools today and the religious teaching of children in some of our modern systems of education leave much to be desired. In the words of B. O. Ukeje (1966), these systems have merely "imparted knowledge without understanding; they have taught the children what to think but not how to think; therefore, students learned to memorize but not digest, to repeat but not to reflect and to adopt even where they should adapt." [5] Internalizing moral values in the children is the only answer to Goleman's question: "how can we bring intelligence to our emotions, civility to our streets and caring to our communal life?" [6] Is either we accept the task and have better-behaved humans for tomorrow or else, the ever increasing moral-deterioration in society.

Generally speaking, our current approach to moral and religious education of children both in the church and schools is rather too shallow and far from ideal. Morality should be taught to children in a deep, involving and enduring manner. It requires much more than the cramming of codes of ethics, laws and standards if morality is to be a prevailing and pervading force in people's lives. As already shown in my treatment of the Igbo family and community life, a true inculcation of moral values demands an endearing relationship with people who are imbibing these values. This mutual relationship must be carried on in ways that are significant, substantial and deeply involving.

For moral education of children to be able to transform those who espouse its value, those who give the education must have definite objectives in mind. They must be sure of the direction they are leading the children. Must know the goals that they want the children to strive after in life. They must map out the standards that they want the children to live up to. Such objectives must be well presented to the children in their training and above all, be exemplified in the lives of those who teach them and in others who relate to the children such as parents and elders. This is where the Igbo-African system of training children is unparalled.

Children In Joint Or Cooperative Education

Throughout human history and civilization, the development of a child's character has been the responsibility, not only of the family but also of the school, the church and the society at large. The school however has had a major role in this regard. This is because young people spend the greater part of their lives within the school walls. There, children will learn either by chance or by design, moral lessons about how people behave. The ultimate goal of the moral lessons is self discipline. Children are influenced by whatever they observe or learn in school either for good or for evil.

"Children," said Roland H. (1974), "need discipline in order to perceive an orderly organized world." The long term objective of discipline according to him is that "individuals become independent, self directing and able to function in a democratic society. This implies that discipline should be reasonable and cooperative rather than arbitrary and autocratic." [7]

The Goal Of Cooperative Education

Moral education should ultimately lead to self discipline. This happens where the home and the school do cooperate, for environment greatly influences behavior. The home is the environment in which the child started his or her life and continues it. When the home and the school unite or cooperate, the things taught in the school are discussed in the home and lived out in the society. This is how maturity in the practice of morality is attained. This is how self discipline is realized. The Parent-Teacher Association meeting becomes a forum where the teachers can discuss with the parents, the need for healthy environments that can encourage moral living.

Both the parents and teachers must come to the understanding that teachers have to act in the place of the parents of the children while in the classroom. Not merely lecturing them but also fathering and mothering them. Not just informing them but also forming them in their character and wholesome maturity.

It is in the school that children "learn to cherish chivalry and truth. There, they learn to pull together, each one with the rest. Playing up and striving, each to do his or her best." [8]

Then will be realized, the sayings of William S. (1975): "The true teacher is one who loves both his children and his subjects. The academic who only loves his students is a traitor. Through it, all should shine the unwavering light of concern for children as persons. About schools in general William said: "Schools have a major role to play in the reclamation of society, and the cultural advancement of homo sapiens. Theirs is the privilege of playing a vital role in preparing each generation to move closer to the point where homo sapiens becomes homo moralis." [9]

My Alma Mater

This is Kings' College, Lagos, Nigeria 1965, which is my Alma Mater. Here I learned to cherish, chivalry and truth. Here, we learned to "pull together, each one with the rest." A child's early school years defines his or her character. And as Heractitus (6th century B.C.) said, "character is destiny." And there can be no destiny without a destination.

Conclusion

The essence of moral education is to influence conduct—the way we interact with one another. Discipline should be the bi-product of moral education, all things being equal. The common pool in which moral education and discipline participate is rules. But rules should not just be given to be memorized. There should be reasons for their establishment. People who keep those rules must be made to see them as reasonable, as they get to understand them.

Those who teach morals need to be educated in both the content and the method of teaching morality in schools. Teachers should be truly dedicated models for children learn faster by imitation. All said and done, the bottom line is that, all who teach morals, must exude morality to be able to impact it. As the ancient Latin dictum puts it: nemo dat, quod non habet (nobody can give, what he or she hasn't got).

Chapter Four

Application Of The Sub-Clinical Therapies In The Rearing Of Children In Today's Modern Society

The Sub-Clinical Therapies

In this last chapter, I have to state that what I have been presenting in this little book together, form what I would call sub-clinical therapies. It should be so-named because our counseling system today is built on diagnosis and treatment of problems in their clinical stages when the symptoms are already manifest. These ancient counseling techniques were in use long ago in almost all cultures of the world especially in the East.

With industrial development and technology, the urbanization processes in most countries and the resultant population drift to towns and cities, the old village communities faded quickly away and with them, these ancient counseling techniques. These great techniques are worth exploring and reclaiming. They certainly can serve as supplements to our modern counseling theories and interventions. When a counselor makes an intake and documents the psycho-social history of a client, that whole update is supposed to lay bare, the sub-clinical role of the family, the community, schools, and churches as well as the organizations that should have been informing, forming, nurturing, and maintaining that client through life. If all these areas of the client's life have been neglected, there is not much that the counselor can do to effect lasting solution to the client's problem.

After the visit to the counselor, the client would still go back to his or her environment to live, school or work. The modern counseling system has been more of a crisis-management scheme. This is comparable to reducing a whole University Teaching Hospital to an Emergency Ward and Intensive Care Unit. These primordial sub-clinical therapies have been there in various forms in all known cultures, long before the advent of our present day counseling methods. They were phased out as nations developed, along with the basic human communities, family systems, clans and villages and the close human interactions that existed in that era.

As herbal medicine and all other forms of health improvement aids are being revived to help the field of medicine today, so can the primordial sub-clinical therapies enrich our counseling in this age. We must therefore take the pains to form human families to intensify our relationships in all life-settings at work, school, and in the society at large. One may see this as a very arduous enterprise in our world and society today, where people want "a quick fix" for everything. This process is not a "push button" matter, but can be facilitated by adapting the rituals, techniques and values described in these first three chapters to each situation and place in time. Basic morality for instance, is simply indispensable for the very survival of the human species on this planet, and children's upbringing is the best ground for its cultivation, and not an intervention scheme.

The incorporation of these ancient therapies will be for counseling, a grass-root device of getting at the root causes of the problems and of staging the battle at the home front of these problems. Counseling will then have both its preventive and its intervention schemes. Counseling is not an intervention, it is life. The counselor's role is to service or do the "tune-up" of the machinery of a client's life in therapy sessions. The counselor should not be expected to provide the right engine parts, the various fluids and lubrication system, the cooling mechanism and other details including the environment in which the engine stays and operates, and its safety. This is the reason why counseling is to be understood as a village or community enterprise.

Children's Upbringing In Today's Modern Society

1. Parenting, In Crisis

Parenting in today's modern society is in serious crisis. Before the 1950's and after, parenting was almost a full time engagement for mothers along with various domestic chores, gardening and even petit trading that can be accommodated by a housewife and mother. Men were often referred to as "breadwinners," as if women were less busy because they were at home.

Today in most families both husband and wife work outside the home, often in distant locations.

With their good salaries, couples can always pay their house maintenance, pay for their children's education and supply all their material needs even more than they dare ask for. Research and experience however show that there can be no substitute for the time that parents must spend interacting and relating with their children. The material goods offered to children cannot take the place of the affection, instructions, dialogues, past times and family meals that parents should share with their children.

As Hillary Clinton (1996) rightly said: "Parenthood has the power to redefine every aspect of life—marriage, work, even relationships with family and friends." [1] This is very true of the Igbo-African family as described in chapters two and three of this book. In the Igbo-African family, the moment the first child arrives into the marriage of a couple, the child's welfare henceforth dictates the life in the family. In that culture, parents live for their children and the children live for their family and harbor their parents in their old age to care for them. Children's experience in the family in their growing years is very crucial for their future. "Families shape our future; our early family experiences heavily influence and to a degree determine how we forever after, think and behave." This is why the upbringing of children is of paramount importance in the Igbo culture.

2. Our Modern Media And Their Addictive Influence In The Family

In some of our modern, perhaps more affluent families today, parents give nourishment to their children, and see to their material needs and academic education. The children's peer group, the school and above all, the media in all its forms and shapes, form their character and shape their lives. Those moments of the day and night, when parents should take time to instruct, guide and caution their children at home have been taken over by the television programs and all the subtle techniques of the media in the society. The parlor has its television and video sets, so has the parents' sleeping rooms as well as the children's rooms.

There is no provision whatever, for the family dialogue and character education of the children. One enters a home in our modern day society only to discover that the television set, like the sorcerer of old, has cast its spell upon everyone; freezing the living into silent statues or else like chattering and clattering birds, so long as the television program lasts. Isn't that amazing! At other instances during the weekends, the entire family as well as their visitors are engrossed in baiting on two football teams for hours. They spend so much of their God-given time debating on the Marlins and the Bulls, the Sharks and the Dolphins! How much time and interest is spent on themselves as husbands and wives and on their children and with their children?

Thus, families have very little time to themselves and for their extended families. Parents find it much easier to let the television, tranquilize their children than form them in customary words of wisdom and direction. Thus, the television has in a way eased the arduous task of caring for and forming children's character. Isn't that as bad as a day care mistress who puts all the babies in her care to sleep by sedating them with Valium rather than nursing and feeding them in the motherly way that she should; simply because she doesn't want to face their troublesomeness! Again, isn't this comparable to the warehousing of the insane in some mental institutions rather than a good treatment and relationship program, which would involve more staffing but would effect their recovery more quickly!

Spouses on their part, often allow the television and the newspapers to usurp that "communion of hearts united in love," which should characterize their lives. Yet, all these could be mere cover-up or fa-cade for growing difficulty in communication between partners. When a couple who had seen each other as most lovely of creatures, worthy of admiration at courtship, can no longer tolerate each other's presence for a good length of time! When they can no longer look into each other's eyes and have a meaningful dialogue, then they should know that something is amiss. It is easy to say "...Well the chase is over, I have bagged the game," as a man once said of his wife. But it is that moment when husbands and wives begin to take each other's worth for granted that their lives begin to elude them. It does not matter how long they are able to cohabit a house and obsess themselves with other issues except the ones that really matter to their family life and union, they are merely "pursing rats while their house is on fire." (Ha n'achu oke, ebe ulo ha n'agba ọku).

The next step would only be for one or both of them to fly to the patronage of some drug, alcohol, or get involved in some secret relationship with another man or woman to complete the chapter and divorce and separation would follow.

3. Children's Video Games And Other Networks

Besides their obsession with the television programs, most children of our sophisticated modern societies today, feed themselves daily and heavily on all sorts of horrible video games, bad enough to distort their personality for life. Some parents are either oblivious of the devastating influence of these video games or have been desensitized themselves from their horror. One of the basic facts of our social life is that you are never neutral in the society. You are either a moulder of the society or you are moulded by the society. As Longfellow put it: "You are either a hammer or an anvil" in the society.

A Los Angeles Times report of November 5, 1993 summarized it thus: "Video games today are dominated by violent themes. Their names give an accurate description: Mortal Kombat, Total Carnage, The Punisher, The Avenger, Vendetta, Street Fighter, Hyper Fighter, Lethal Enforcer. In these games, children take on the roles of characters like Captain Carnage or Major Mayhem. The predominant goal is to kill or maim an opponent by gouging, smashing, pummeling, shooting, vaporizing. The winner is the one who kills the greatest number of people.

Children learn a lot of evil promptings from these games and they experiment on them in some ways. Believe it or not, large doses of vicarious violence will condition these children in some degree to accept real violence as one of the solutions to life's problems. These games could fuel a killer instinct in some of them. Some kids who have a steady diet of playing violent video games may become more aggressive with other children in real world or more intolerant of the aggressions around them."

"The average child in the U.S. today," said B. Spock, "has watched 8000 depictions of murder before finishing elementary school, and each viewing makes the child more callous." [2] Compare this whole atmosphere of children's life with the earlier account that I have of my personal experience of growing up in my family. Here in the modern society and family, the most gruesome, violent videos have replaced the moral and religious education from parents and elders. We rivaled one another as siblings in practicing the virtues which we learned from our parents and our elders and the community.

4. The Work Situation

The system of work in the more developed nations of the world today is the greatest single factor that militates against any meaningful interaction of family members. I once put a question to a group of acquaintances by the first month of my stay here in the United States; I asked: "Are relatives here, really related?" In unison they said, "Oh yes, of course, we are." "I don't see much of it personally," I said. "How often do you see one another, hold family meetings, visit family members and demonstrate your common bond as a family and kin?"

"Come on! Father Greg," said someone in the group, "we do it all by phone even from work, we don't need to visit physically for lack of time but each person understands the pressure of work; two jobs, three jobs! We also have the annual get together for Thanksgiving Day and Memorial Day and Christmas!." Those answers were not satisfactory for me of course. Many people in today's modern world live in lonely crowds from day to day and year to year."

The telephone is certainly not a substitute for the physical contacts and interaction of people knit together by the natural bond of love and blood. It may work for a few, but for the majority, there is need for greater union. "The Internet, fax, and e-mail have added to our facilities but only help to make us less visible and touchable in our impersonal relationships, while many have become addicts of these facilities in today's global village" (Richard Emeka Nwaobi 2000). Who then should be surprised at the many broken marriages many dysfunctional families, given to drugs, alcohol, gambling, sexual promiscuity, and other addictions and the myriad of pathologies that plague our modern societies!

My criticism of the injudicious use of these modern communication links should not be misunderstood. They are all wonderful means of communication, of information, and relaxation. They are however no substitutes for the physical touch and celebration of the very gift, that we are to one another. Human life is emptied of its substance and meaning, the less relationship we have with others and with God. Nature abhors a vacuum, and emptiness of relationships, beget aparty in people and the urge to relate unnaturally, or with the wrong person or things.

A meaningful relationship with God is even more crucial for our physical and mental well being. Thus, Carl Jung (1961) could say, "There is a purposeful center of reality with which man needs to be in conscious contact for his full health. Man is seldom in sound physical and mental health, unless he can find some way to relate to this center of being whom he calls God." [3] Jung's position is a crucial reality of human existence, emphasizing our dependency on God as contingent creatures. Not to have a functioning relationship with God in the family life would mean chaos and disintegration. It is when people neglect or lose touch with this center of their being that they in vain drift to the wrong persons and things that will never satisfy their yearning. St. Augustine (A.D. 354-430), got it right when he said: "Lord, you have made us for yourself; and our hearts are restless, till they rest in Thee."

Freedom And Discipline Among The Youth In Our Modern Society

Many teenagers and young adults in our modern societies of today certainly have the wrong concept of freedom. They had no disciplinary training growing up, and have been ill informed on what freedom, truly is. A few examples will make this point clear. I met a woman recently in a program who proudly announced to the group that she was going to have her fourth wedding ceremony. The people around me were each congratulating her and wishing her "happy wedding" when she said: "I already have three children from my previous marriage and I hope this one works out fine. I am free to marry as many times as I like. It's all my decision and I should live my life as I want . . ." I was simply stunned! What will be the fate of those children from perhaps three or two different fathers? What will be their own understanding of marriage and family as they grow up? Who will give them the formation that should mould their character and personality?

Some teenagers today believe they can marry whoever, wherever, and whenever they like and jump out of the union when and how they like. For them, sex and marriage are adventures and fun, and fun is insanity. A little tune that I used to hear in our Rehab Center runs thus: "I don't care, who you are, where you from, what job you do, as long as you love me . . ." This tune is supposed to be a love tune. Now, a marriage that would not consider a partner's personality, ethnicity nor job but only "Love" as a criterion is built on very thin air. The crucial question here is, what really is married love? Does it mean instant sexual gratification and momentary infatuation with the physical appearance of someone and empty sentiments?

All that some young people have as their weapon and guide today are: "I have my life to live. I am free to live my life as I want. I have to be me and what I do is nobody's business . . ." People with this frame of mind also believe that their lives are their private property which they can preserve or destroy at will. Whether they do this by direct acts of suicide or destroy themselves with drugs, illicit sex, and the diseases that could be transmitted through it, is nobody's business. All they know is that they are exercising their liberty. We know however that there is no human act that does not affect someone else, directly or indirectly especially in the family setting. One needs to be present in a family counseling session to see how the addictive life of a single member of the family whether a parent or child can infect and enslave the rest of the family even intergenerationally!

An Example: What greater tragedy can there be, than the case of a youth that I once visited in the hospital here, who became the father of a child at the age of fifteen through a teenage girl. At seventeen, he had a second child by another girl. By his 20th birthday, he was already a victim of the almighty AIDS. Most likely any of those babies he fathered could be HIV positive. In a discussion with the youth in the hospital one day he said: "When I was a boy, I was very handsome and girls were falling for me. I had all the freedom I wanted at home and so, I was smoking cigarettes and taking my buzz already at the age of eleven, when I went for parties or had dates. It was all fun you know..." This was his explanation for the undisciplined life he had lived. He died soon after, at the age of twenty-one. What a life of woes. Family upbringing and the wrong concept of freedom are in question here.

The Right Approach

In their years of adolescence, children naturally push for greater liberty as they struggle with the crisis of their emerging personalities and identity, in their psychosocial development. They however need the guidance of parents and elders at this stage, more than ever. In some of our modern societies of today, where the laws of individual's rights and freedom often favor the children wrongly, parents, elders and other lawfully constituted authorities like the schools, are handicapped. Their hands are simply tied and children in their exercise of "freedom" ruin themselves.

The Igbo-African systemic culture has a radically different approach to this. There is a powerful Igbo axiom which states: "Afu akaghi, n'egbu okenye; akaa anughi n'egbu nwata." (An elder's negligence of his or her duty to reprimand and instruct the youth, causes his or her death, while the youth's refusal to heed the instruction of the elder kills him or her). This axiom is a societal norm of the Igbo systemic culture which shows that both the young and the old are mutually bound to live out the laws and values of the society. The culture empowers not only parents, elders and other authorities, to discipline, guide and protect the young from both physical and spiritual ills, but also enjoins even older siblings, to correct and protect the younger, in the family.

Thus, an elder who sees a youth sneaking around outside his or her parent's home at night and does not reprimand or even punish the youth on the spot, has failed in his or her civic duty and proved a traitor to his or her older age and so, is liable to punishment by his or her own conscience. The youth who fails to heed instruction or warning of the elder would ultimately die or get into serious trouble from breaking the law some day.

We should notice here that the elder who punished or reprimanded the "sneaking" youth did not ask: "whose child are you?" The simple fact is that he or she is nwaobodo (child of the village) his or her problem is a village problem, which every villager should be obliged to solve and be concerned with.

Now, compare this mutual obligation of the young and the old to uphold socially approved behaviors and morals, to the current trend in our modern individualistic societies. Any correction given to a child in our western "freedom" cultures today could be labeled "child-abuse". It could be termed, verbal, emotional or mental abuse! How then can misbehaviors be discouraged in children?

Communalism Versus Individualism

The Igbo-African communal lifestyle is based on the systemic theory and philosophy. As shown in the last two chapters, the systemic lifestyle sees individuals in the society always in context of relationship to others, not in isolation. Human life operations among the Igbos is always relationally, contextually, and interactionally situated.

Our great ancestors in the old cultures were able to survive their near-stone-age era because they maintained this systemic lifestyle. An example of this mutual cooperation and close relationship style of life may be helpful here: In the African villages many years ago, people fetched their fire each day from a neighborhood home in the early morning, afternoon, or evening to cook their meals. Matches or lighters were not common then. It only needed one family to light fire by striking or rubbing two granite stones in a trash of dry leaves, to make fire. The rest of the neighborhood or community would gradually fetch fire that day by looking up to see where some smoke is coming off a house roof, to fetch their fire, with some raffia palm or bambo stick.

The first person who lit the fire in the day, loses none of his or her fire by allowing the fire to spread to all the other homes in that village. Instead, that person is happy and better fulfilled that more people have been served and could in turn be going to any of those homes to borrow a rope or pail, to draw water from the village cistern. This spirit of sharing, and of joy in serving the community or humanity, is a very scarce commodity, in the world markets, of today's individualistic-capitalistic societies.

Moral Implications Of The Communal Spirit

A very important moral lesson that we need to note in the communal spirit of this old culture is this: Nobody ever felt puffed up or elated by what he or she had. What you are and what you have are for the community's pride, and for service. The joy of having, is in serving and giving to others. Possessions and acquisitions whether stated explicitly or not, are understood as being and existing for the good and honor of the community essentially, more than for the self-aggrandizement of the individual who has them. A village civic hall, a village cistern or well, the granite stone at the center of a family compound or village, each serves the entire people who use the hall for meetings, fetch water from the well, or sharpen their knives on the stone. They are part of the group's identity. Each of these items is an honor to the whole group and serves their need and pride.

In like manner, if a wealthy man in a village erects a great mansion, buys a Lorry or has an electric plant that gives light to his compound and some other homes around him, the entire village take pride in the mansion, the Lorry or the electric plant. The joy that is shared by all is that this man is **"OUR"** son! This mansion or house is in **"OUR"** village. That generator is booming in **"OUR"** community. It is the mark of systemic or communal lifestyle to share life's earnings, life's joys and sorrows. The life in this system is based on St. Paul's injunction to the church in Rome when he said: "Rejoice with those who rejoice; weep with those who weep" (Roman 12:15). Thus in the Igbo systemic culture, "nothing is fully possessed, except it is shared." The joy of one is the joy of all. No one feels dissatisfied or envious that the generator is not in his own compound. Nobody feels disgruntled that the great mansion was better placed if it had been his personal house. Thus, when the women are dancing and rejoicing at the birth of a new baby, they sing a lyric that says: "Whoever gives birth, should take her turn in rejoicing and let all join her. Someday too, it will be my turn and I shall rejoice, while you all will join me to rejoice!" They do not envy other's progress. In general, people in this systemic culture do not begrudge anyone for what he or she has nor do they feel contemptuous towards those who have not. Their belief system teaches them that nobody is absolutely self-sufficient. Thus the Igbo-Africans would call a child the name Uwaezuoke (no one is all self-sufficient in life). In common speech, they pose it as a question. (Who is ever all sufficient as not to need anyone or lack anything in his or her life?)

In the traditional communal life of the Igbos therefore, how far a good benefits the generality or greater number of people, is what counts.

Interdependency And Mutual Relationship Is A Necessity For Humans

The numerous inquiries of science especially of paleontology, have abundant proof for the fact that the various species of animal life lived together according to their classes. Part of the explanation for their gregarious nature was certainly their need for coexistence, interdependency and interaction, all for their necessary survival. No one therefore doubts the fact that the original tendency of humans was that of interrelatedness.

The Birth Of Individualism

From the dawn of human history till the lapse of the medieval epoch about 1500 A.D., people still acknowledged globally that humans could best realize their full potentials in relationship with others. Both existentialism and phenomenology espoused this in their teachings both in the East and the West. Later, in an effort to guard against the "dissolution" of the individual in interrelationships, and interdependency with others, western philosophy over-emphasized the "absolute originality and concreteness of the human person as a 'being for itself.'" Thus, that perpendicular pronoun the "I," was absolutized! It's autonomy and incommunicability was fundamental to personhood.

This was the genesis of the modern notion of the human person as "an individual of sheer autonomous will, whose life is the sole development of his or her personality." "I have got to be me!" it is either me or nothing else is." This is the idolized "self," the enthronement of individualism. In their sociological research book, "Habits of the Heart," Robert N. Bellah and his colleagues pointed out some of the implications of this individualism and personalism in the American life: "The dignity and sacredness of the individual are seen in American culture today as the inviolable right to think, judge, and make decisions for oneself and live one's life as one sees fit. Any infringement of this right is not only morally wrong (an abuse) but also "sacrilegious."

Even a seven year old kid in the American society of today knows that the hands of parents, elders, and the school teachers are somehow tied by the now undefined right and freedom given to the individual in an individualistic society. Thus, R. N. Bellah and his colleagues could write: "...If the individual is prior to the society and if society emerges through the voluntary contract of individuals trying to maximize their self interest, then, the survival of both society and individual becomes problematic." [4] We notice that the part is greater than the whole in this system. What an anomaly, for the cover of the container to be larger than the container itself! But as an Igbo-African axiom has it: alu gba afor, obulu omenala (when an abomination or anomaly perdures over a long period, it becomes a tradition). Thus, that which is intrinscially an anomaly and an aberration, has become a tradition in some cultures today.

Reclaiming The "Self" For Society

When a person circumscribes his world to himself, to whatever powers he can wield in various areas of life for his personal comfort and convenience, tastes and interests, it is precisely then that his world becomes empty. Even the relationships he contracts, all are impersonal and empty. He then lives in fear, anxiety and distrust of everyone including himself deep within. The only counseling that can help this individualistic person is to reconnect him to his "family extensions" and help him to take his rightful place in the society and the church, to be truly a functioning member of his world of being. His openness to others in the society and the caring acceptance that he will receive in return, will heal him from inside out, till he becomes an integrated personality, fully human, giving and receiving love from others.

Examined closely, individualistic persons are unfulfilled people with deep yearning for human warmth and intimacy but with deeper fear and distrust for others and therefore, afraid to be involved in any meaningful commitment with society.

The Good Old Days, And The Good Old Ways

Elderly people in all cultures, often wish for a return to their teen years; a nostalgia for what they call, "the good old days." They have this longing because the order and harmony that prevailed in human society in their growing years, is seriously lacking today. Above all, discipline and morality are at a very low ebb and the revered traditional values, spiritual and social norms, that governed human life, are rare to come by in our time. The dignity and sacredness of the human person for the bare fact of being human and not for what he or she has, has been violated. Ours, is now a culture of violence, of deception and addiction.

The elderly people were in the old dispensation, accorded awesome respect and were so dearly loved and appreciated for their venerable grey hair. They had the honor of sages, were the custodians of the moral law and served as consultants, mediators of peace, justice and reconciliation in their families and in the societies at large. Therefore, they felt needed, useful, beloved and had a sense of belonging to their communities. Today, unfortunately, many elderly people, unless they are wealthy, are neglected and seen as unproductive and of little account. Their children and grandchildren may not take them into their homes to reciprocate the care that they themselves had received. The elderly see so much violence, immorality and deceit in our world that they yearn to be freed from this world of scandal, and that explains their longing for the "good old days."

The Old Brigade And The Good Old Ways

In diverse cultures today, elderly people or "The Old Brigade," who in their "wishful thinking" recall their "good old days," are indeed re-echoing the standards set by their predecessors and which they lived out in their growing years. Such standards have changed radically today.

America for example is one of the great nations of the world that based their existence and government on God, religion, morality and discipline at their inception. That so much importance was placed on these values and on the character of individuals could be seen from the proclamations of some of their founding fathers. Thus, at his inaugural speech, George Washington (1789), the first President of American said: "...the foundations of our national policy will be laid in the pure and immutable principles of private morality." By this, Washington is implying that it is the collective output of individual family lives that determines the moral order and discipline in the community, the society or nation. Yet, the root of the indiscipline and moral depravity in today's world and society stems from the "undefined" freedom that individualistic persons and nations claim. It was not so with America in the beginning.

Writing to his cousin in 1776, John Adams said: "It is only religion and morality that can establish the principles upon which freedom can securely stand." As if to explain why it is only religion and morality that can establish the principles upon which the freedom accorded America can stand, John Adams (1798) while serving as America's second President said: "Our Constitution was made only for a moral and religious people. It is wholly inadequate to the government of any other." Now, we need to answer the question: "Why is it inadequate for any other except Americans who are governed by moral and religious principles!"

First of all, we have to note from his pronouncements that the freedom that is embedded in the American Constitution, was both defined by, and dependent upon religion and morality for its operation or exercise. Those who abuse that freedom in America today, see it as a license for insanity and immorality. Alexis de Tocqueville (1832) answered the above question so well when he said: "While the constitutional law of liberty allowed Americans complete freedom to do as they pleased, religion PREVENTED them from doing that which was immoral and unjust." Continuing, Tocqueville said: "Without the moral restrictions of a higher spiritual law, the liberty afforded Americans in the Constitution would be abused." [5] The above view is similar to my summary statement for Chapter One of this book: "Unless there is within us, a moral law and order, mightier than the conflicts which are outside us, we will soon yield to the forces around and about us." Only self-discipline or conscientization can keep one on the path of law and order here. It is quite obvious now that the freedom granted to those who would live by religion and morality is being abused today, by those who no longer live by religion and morality. Imposition of laws external to the individual is no solution. Only thorough moral and disciplinary education can reform people, not force or drugs.

The Family Environment

We need to understand that the youths today are what their environment made them. The family and community have much of the answer for the behavior of children in today's world. Marriages nowadays are so unstable, ending more often in divorce than ever before in all human history. If we are to be true to statistics, it would be more accurate for couples who make their marriage vows in church or court in our sophisticated societies today, to say rather, "...till divorce do us part." Since they are too much in a haste to wait for death to severe the bond.

The family has become a school of scandal for many children today. As Hillary Clinton observed "divorce constitutes 40% of American children's major life stress. By 1960," said she, "one in every twenty children in American was born out of wedlock, but today, it is one in every four."[6] Researches show that children living with one parent or in step families are two to three times as likely to have emotional and behavioral problems as children living in two parent families." Beside marriages being unstable in our time, the very entrance of children into our world today is often the genesis of the behavioral problems that they exhibit throughout life in some cases.

As we saw in the Igbo-African system, children are already claimed by their community while yet in the womb and all measures are taken to protect them from any harm. On the contrary, many children nowadays are brain-damaged in-utero through parents' carelessness in their use of drugs. "The National Institute of Drug Abuse estimates that 500,000 women of child bearing age used cocaine in 1990. Also, the National Drug Control Policy estimates that 100,000 cocaine exposed infants are borne each year, many with serious health problems such as low birth weight, brain damage and neurological and respiratory problems. It is now an established fact that a baby exposed to cocaine in-utero, will experience withdrawal symptoms at birth. The baby will be irritable, jittery, unresponsive, and difficult to comfort. This unresponsiveness from the infant, coupled with the guilt that a mother may feel for using drugs before her child's birth, can make bonding difficult."

Far worse than the children whose family life experience were so discouraging are those children who could not have the opportunity of living with any of their parents but must live in foster homes. "About 450,000 children are in our foster care system at any given time and close to 100,000 of them will not be reunited with their families." [7] Now, as one steps out of the immediate nuclear family, we think of our extended family members who help in the moulding of the character of children and are part of their world even after they have got married with families of their own. The urbanization system, the materialistic tendencies and business ethics of today's world, has torn down the walls of what used to form a child's family extensions. You ask some people in our top modern societies today about their families, the answers you get are simply bizarre and most discouraging. It is then that one begins to wonder if indeed, relatives are still related, in our modern societies!

Not only do children lose touch with their extended family members, they rarely have lasting peers, school teachers or homely neighbors that they can count on, long enough to know them well because of the frequent moves of parents. What a nomadic life where people cannot hope of having friends and long time neighbors and acquaintances!

Use Of Drugs By Infants And Children In Today's Society

Over 2.5 million children in the United States use behavioral drugs. Can anything be more alarming and unfortunate! The excuse that is often given for this massive destruction of children's future is that these children are on drugs because they have behavioral problems. If the problems are behavioral, that means, relational and interactional; then, human relationship techniques should be used for them and not drugs. After all, parents of some of these children do have marital problems which take them to counseling. Those problems are often relational, the key to which could be communication problems between the partners. The counselors do not prescribe behavioral drugs for those couples. Rather, they help them to learn good communication.

Psychotropic drugs such as Ritalin, Prozac, and Luvox are so easily recommended for children in schools nowadays. For parents to put their children on drugs prescribed commonly for attention deficit and hyperactive disorders is to say the least, unfair if not criminal. Attention deficit and hyperactive disorders most often are problems requiring behavioral trainings, discipline and education. A few of them could genuinely be neurological and so, needing prescriptions by doctors, and not teachers or parents. Disordered behavior can be overcome by ordered behavior. Each is a learned process, and there are no "quick fix" for them. The New York Times of November 24, 1999 reported the case of a school girl who was showing signs of attention deficit disorder through mood sweeps and napping in class. A teacher had said to the girl's parents: "You need to get her a prescription for Ritalin." Later, the girl was diagnosed with hypoglycemia and needed to change her diet. This is an example of what I mean by that urge for a "quick fix" in today's society.

Imagine teachers giving ultimatum to parents: "Put your kids on a drug or we are not going to teach them." Such teachers should do better in the drug companies than in the classrooms.

Further Inquiries Into The Use Of Psychotropic Drugs By Kids

It is necessary to ask the question, why do some teachers insist that the supposed hyperactive or attention deficit kids be put on drugs? The issue here is that such kids are classified as "at risk students" by the teachers, to justify the recommendation of drugs for them. This then is like "giving a dog a bad name in order to hang it."

As Nathan (1991) puts it: "Labeling students as 'at risk' can set in motion, a vicious self-fulfilling prophecy. No matter how well meaning, targeted programs that label children as 'at risk' may be doing more harm than good. The term 'at risk' is unfounded and unrealistic. It defines a child as pathological, based on what he or she might do rather than on anything he or she has actually done."

When people are labeled as "at risk" or are given any other stigma like telling a child, "Look, you are not going to be of much use in life;" the child may think or feel himself or herself into a full blown image of this odious picture, painted of him or her by parents, teachers or elders to make that label realized. "Oh, I am said to be useless, and so I am! I am 'a no-do-well" and so—why do I need to go on trying? After all I am destined to failure!" Thus, the person struggles to accept the label or to reject it. If accepted, it is also internalized. The label takes over the personality and suppresses his or her ego! We do somehow strive to become what we are named. If it can be suggested to you that you are a very strong man, a great weight-lifter for instance, and that there is no limit to what weight you can bear; by accepting and internalizing this attribute as yours, you can lift a weight perhaps, two times than normal. The reverse is equally true as we have already seen in the case of the "no-do-well-child."

Conversely, when in the Igbo-African system of children's character formation, elders, or parents notice a child who is really problematic, rascally or hyperactive, all they would say is: Ara kasi nma na okorobia (madness is best in youth). Once said or acknowledged, they would give this child more attention than others. They take measures to encourage and to tap the child's little talents and interests and from there help him or her to be more law abiding, responsible and self controlled. They would be both soft and firm in the training and would exhaust their patience till the child is reformed and transformed with the passage of time. They do not look for a "quick fix."

My Personal Experiences

In my early childhood days, I could be classified as really hyperactive, as that term goes today. I was always excited to be with my parents and elder brothers and sisters in the farm during the planting season for instance. In the farm, I was running up and down from one section of the farm to the other, doing whatever little weeding, cleaning or gathering I was allowed to do. I would climb little shrubs and trees, fall or get wounded in the thorns and thistles, and run back to my Dad crying. He would always solace and encourage me not to be "all over the farm which of course, I would not heed. He did not stop bringing me to the farm, rather, after consoling me whenever I got wounded, he would send me back to the work saying: "go back to work my son, don't be discouraged nor be afraid because of your falls and wounds, a lion does not give birth to a cowardly cur (agu anaghi amu nwa ujo).

Again, when I began my seminary training for the priesthood, I was then quite rascally and so quick tempered. One of the priest formators often caught me in the very act of trying to fight whenever I was upset in the soccer field. On such occasions, I would report at his office after, expecting to be suspended or expelled as the rules prescribed. All that this priest would say to me was ". . . Look Greg, you have to grow up . . . The church needs some mad men and you are one of them, so, go your way and don't do that again." He did not send me home as a quick solution. He rather helped me to direct all those energies and temper to music and other creative interests as I worked slowly on my temperament for good.

Yet, some one can argue that these assertions of the Igbos is a form of labeling. It is not. Rather, it shows that the Igbo culture has from centuries of moulding and modeling children's character, realized that some children do have some traits or tendencies that must be worked on to trim them to the ideal behavior that society upholds. It is their own way of diagnosing the problem of the youth and yet making light of it for in some cases, the child is just being his or her age. Thus the Igbos would say: Ogbede n'eto (The young shall grow). They bear patiently with the problematic child as they form him or her, for they are aware that the children are not in a hurry as we adults are.

Developing A Moral Culture In Today's Modern Society

There is no need to take refuge in the belief that today's culture is that of violence; no need to believe that the society is irremediably corrupt for children to live morally good lives in it. As that Igbo-African axiom puts it: Madu bu njo ala and conversely, Madu bu nma ala (Humans make the society either good or bad). We make the world. In any human society, one is either a moulder of society or is moulded by the society. You either involve yourself actively to influence the society for the better or remain the passive victim of whatever others bring to bear on the society.

If all in a given community make morality and discipline their goal, that community is sure to breathe the pure air that is morally uncontaminated. It is only when any arm of the society goes on to pervert those standards or sabotage them, that the goals will not be realized. It needs the unanimous cooperation of all in the society, to effect a moral order. Stringent measures must be taken against parents, teachers, and any person or group that does not cooperate in such matters. Only self centeredness and self interest either in any individual or group, can destroy such community effort. To reclaim the traditional values, the morality and discipline that characterized the "good old days." We must follow the Igbo-African approach described in this book. It is all summarized in the saying: Onye na egbo Ogu, gbo nra (He who would stop a fight, should do well to discourage all who in any way, instigate or insinuate fighting). It is a preventive approach rather than an intervention. It deals with the problem, ever before it builds up. It "nips the problem in the bud." The intervention approach which is our traditional counseling approach is crisis management scheme or stopping the fight after it has begun. The flaws in this system are obvious: Injuries have already been suffered by a victim or victims and even though counseling tries to heal the wounds, the scars would still remain as reminders and source of possible renewal of the wound in future. Therefore a prevention of the wound is too priceless to compare with the best intervention that can be given after the fight. The fighters lose their reputation in the society and so do their families. The impulse to fight has been instilled with that first attempt at fighting. On the other hand, the Igbo-African upbringing of children inclines a child more to seek peace than war, more to flight than to fight and more to construction than to destruction. The training instills good naturedness in the child. Then, their systemic lifestyle is meant to preserve, nurture, and favor that nature in the child throughout life.

Most of the behavioral problems of children today could have been forestalled by parents and those that made up the world in which the children grew up. Children would have been victors rather than the victims of most of today's social ills. When the moral values that children have imbibed are practiced perseveringly and handed on from generation to generation, only then can the good old ways turn our time to the good old days. Habit is formed through repetitive acts.

The Place Of The Counselor, In The Sub-Clinical Therapy Scheme

Some colleagues, have often asked me in counseling as well as in Moral Theology classes, "what I think would be the role of the professional counselor if the issues that are treated in counseling today can be resolved by the primordial counseling methods that I often talked about. The answer to this question is simply that professional counselors will then serve as consultants, coordinators and animators in the whole counseling enterprise. Then will professional counseling be well supplemented, more effective, less energy-draining and more enjoyable. The sub-clinical therapies cannot, and are not meant to substitute professional counseling today because, these primordial therapies were able to handle the problems of the past effectively in a world and society that was quite simple. People were then, closely knit together as families and communities.

Today, our world and society have become very complex and many people have become equally very individualistic and selfish. The more people know, today, the less they believe and cooperate with one another in the essential values and virtues of human life. Cordial human interaction is becoming more and more difficult. Human relationship problems, which are basically the ground of counseling today have grown in geometrical progression through the years. Religion and moral education especially of children were among the basic tools for training in human behavior. Today, these have been discarded in most of our "modern sophisticated societies" and we are paying dearly for this. As

Theodore Roosevelt (1901-1909) warned long ago, "to educate a person in mind and not in morals, is to educate a menace to society."

In 1940 when the radio network conducted a survey about discipline-concerns in the schools, the seven top problems were: talking, chewing gum, making noise, running in the halls, getting out of turn in line, wearing improper clothing, and not putting paper in the waste basket. When the study was replicated in 1980, the seven top problems were: drug abuse, robbery and assault, arson, gang warfare, and venereal diseases. If we compare the two periods with the situation in our present day society, we would admit that the situation demands much more than counseling interventions. In past histories, people were much more easily content with what they had, who they were and where they were in their lives journey in the society. Today, people are becoming more and more insatiable, as many are out to have not what they really need, but what they want! That old Latin proverb is so true to our age, which said: "armo habendi, habendo grescit" (the love of having, increases the desire for having). In other words, the more we have, the more we would still like to have.

Ideally, the counseling program should aim at the "total health" of clients. This "total health" should guarantee that the client's world of existence is wholly healthy. The client can best attain this state in the midst of other healthy people all of whom can help the client to remain healthy. It would mean, living among healthy family members, in a healthy community, healthy schoolmates or fellow workers and associates. This certainly cannot be realized unless our present day counseling scheme can incorporate the sub-clinical therapies as an integral dimension of the whole counseling scheme.

The golden age of the counseling enterprise, will therefore be set in motion with the orientation of people in all cultures, always to see the larger picture of life in all its settings.

In this global village of today's world, many people live simply in their little worlds and always see things subjectively from their "personal world of reality" and may not care whether other people outside their "world circumscription" survive or not! Our global village has effected greater neighborhood but very little brotherhood. Morris Maddocks (1981) was of the above view when he wrote: "I am unhealthy, however brilliant my mind, and fit my body, if from the comfortable chair in my living room, I can watch my brothers and sisters in the third world, starve or destroy themselves in violent efforts to obtain the bare necessities of life." [8] The above is applicable to counseling which is a quest for mental health and healing. But health and healing are all universal symbols or attributes affected by, and affecting the whole of creation. We cannot separate the client's health from his or her world of existence. The counseling program therefore can thrive best in a communal rather than an individualistic background. Counseling is of necessity, a family and community venture and not just the business of the client and counselor.

Notes

Prologue

1. Elochukwu E. Uzukwu, A Listening Church: Autonomy and Communion in African Churches. (New York: Orbis Books,1996), p. 43.
2. E. I. Metuh, African Religion in Western Conceptual Schemes. (Ibadan Pastoral Institute, 1985), p. 262.
3. Elochukwu E. Uzukwu, p. 37.

Introduction

1. Mary B. McRae, Delores A. Thompson, and Sharon Cooper, "Black Churches As Therapeutic Groups." Journal Of Multi-Cultural Counseling and Development, (Vol. 27 No.4), pg. 207.

Chapter One

1. M. O. Onwuemelie, The Influence of Christian Religion On Igbo Personality. (Unpublished Thesis submitted in partial fulfillment of the requirement for Bachelor's Degree in Theology, Bigard Memorial Seminary, Enugu, 1978), p. 35.
2. Henry Bettenson, The Early Christian Fathers. (London: Oxford University Press, 1956), p. 104.
3. F. A. Arinze, Sacrifice in Igbo Religion. (Ibadan University Press, 1970), p. 8.
4. J. P. Jordan, Bishop Shanahan of Southern Nigeria. (Dublin: ELO Press Ltd., 1949), p. 117.
5. Morris Maddocks, The Christian Healing Ministry. (London: Dotesios Printers Ltd., 1990), p. 5.

6. J. S. Mbiti, The Prayers of Africa. (London: SPCK, 1975), p. 7.

7. G. T. Basden, Among The Igbos Of Nigeria. (London: Frank Cass and Co. Ltd., 1966), p. 215.

8. V. C. Uchendu, The Igbo Of South Eastern Nigeria. (New York: Holt, Rinehart & Winston, 1965), p. 96.

9. M. M. Green, Igbo Village Affairs 2nd ed. (London: Frank Cass and Co. Ltd., 1964), p. 100.

10. F. A. Arinze, p. 15.

11. Robert B. Ewen, Introduction To Theories of Personality 4th ed. (1993), p. 89.

12. E. Idowu Bolaji, African Traditional Religion. (London: SCM Press, 1975), p. 179.

13. Dorothy S. Becvar and Raphael J. Becvar, Family Therapy: A Systemic Integration. (Allyn and Bacon, Inc. 1996), p. 149.

14. Edwin Smith, African Ideas of God. (London: Edinburgh House Press, 1961), p. 117.

15. Kathryn P. Shimabukuro, Judy Daniels, and Michael D. Andrea, "Addressing Spiritual Issues From A Cultural Perspective."In the Journal of Multicultural Counseling (Vol. 27 No. 4), p. 221.

16. Hines and Boyd Franklin, "Spirituality and Therapy." Ibid., p. 241.

17. Anderson and Worthen, Ibid., p. 243.

18. Aponte (1994) and Walsh (1998), Ibid., p. 243.

19. Timothy E. O'Connell, Principles for a Catholic Morality. (New York: Harper, Collins Publishers, 1990), p. 134.

20. Michael Bertram Crowe, The Changing Profile Of The Natural Law. (The Hague Netherlands, 1977), p. 3

21. Ibid., pp. 37-41.
22. Ibid., pp. 141-142.
23. Timothy E. O'Connell, Ibid., pp. 109-110.

Chapter Two

1. Hillary Rodham Clinton, It Takes A Village and Other Lessons Children Teach Us. (New York: Simon and Schuster, Inc., 1996), p. 12.
2. Gerald Corey, Theory And Practice of Counseling and Psychotherapy. (New York: Books/Cole Publishing Company, 1996), p. 367.
3. Dorothy S. Becvar et. al., Ibid., p. 149.
4. Gerald Corey, Ibid., pp137-138.
5. Timothy E. O'Connell, Ibid., p. 162.
6. John C. Cavanaugh and Robert V. Kall, Human Development, (California: Brooks/Cole Publishing Co., 1996), p. 44.
7. Paul Bohannan and Philip Curtins, Africa and Africans. (New York: Natural History Press, 1971), p. 116.
8. Dorothy S. Becvar, et. al., Ibid, p. 125.

Chapter Three

1. R. J. Harrison, Environment and Politics in West Africa. (Canada: D. Van Nostrand Co., Inc., 1963), p. 110.
2. Ron Brandt, Journal of Educational Leadership (Vol. 51, 1993), p. 621.
3. Sylvia Hewlett, Ibid., (Vol. 51 No. 2), pp. 63-80.
4. Barbara Dafoe Whitehead, Ibid., p. 531.
5. B. O. Ukeje, Education For Social Reconstruction. (Nigeria: Lagos MacMillan and Company Ltd., 1966), p. 60.

6. Daniel Goleman (Hillary Rodham Clinton), Ibid., p. 9.
7. Roland E. Briggs, <u>The Relationship Between Religion and Moral Education</u>. (West African Journal of Education, No. 18), p. 86.
8. "King's College. Lagos, Nigerian School Anthem," 1965.
9. J. S. William, "Education in Schools Today." West African Journal Of Education, 1974, No. 18.

Chapter Four

1. Hillary Rodham Clinton, Ibid., p. 9.
2. B. M. Spock, <u>A Better World For Our Children: Rebuilding American Family Values</u>. (Chicago: Contemporary Books Publishing Co., 1994), p. 76.
3. Morris Maddocks, Ibid., p. 39.
4. Elochukwu E. Uzukwu, Ibid., pp. 43-44.
5. Gerald and Stephen Flurry, <u>Character in Crisis</u>. (Philadelphia Church of God, 1998), pp 3 – 12
6. Hillary, Rodham Clinton Ibid., p. 39.
7. Hillary Rodham Clinton, Ibid., p. 47.
8. Morris Maddocks, Ibid., p. 5.

About The Author

Father Greg Udo Njoku, C. S. Sp, is a Catholic Priest of the Province of Nigerian Holy Ghost Fathers. He is currently a student of Barry University, Miami, Florida, U.S.A.

Father Greg holds a Master's degree in Pastoral Theology with specialty in Mental Health Counseling and Family Therapy.

Father Greg Udo Njoku, C. S. Sp
(305) 860-9248